HOW TO START AND RUN A USED BOOK STORE:

A Book Store Owner's Essential Toolkit with Real-World Insights, Strategies, Forms, and Procedures

STEPHANIE CHANDLER

How to Start and Run a Used Book Store:
A Book Store Owner's Essential Toolkit with Real-World Insights, Strategies, Forms, and Procedures
By Stephanie Chandler
1. Business and Economics: Entrepreneurship 2. Business and Economics: New Business Enterprises 3. Antiques and Collectibles: Books

ISBN: 978-1-935953-00-5

Original Copyright © 2006 by Stephanie Chandler
Revised Edition

Cover Design by Connie Cong

Printed in the United States of America

Authority Publishing
11230 Gold Express Dr. #310-413
Gold River, CA 95670
800-877-1097
www.AuthorityPublishing.com

Table of Contents

Introduction

When I told my colleagues, family, and friends that I was opening a used book store, most of them looked at me as if my hair were on fire. Many mercilessly asked, "How are you going to make a living doing *that*?" I had worked in the Silicon Valley for a decade and had a successful career in software sales. But the demands of that work gave me an ulcer before my thirtieth birthday and a burning desire (literally!) to find work that I loved.

I have always been a bookworm and I frequent book stores at every opportunity. While I was desperately searching for ideas to get me out of the high stress of corporate America, it suddenly occurred to me that I would love to run my own used book store.

I immediately began to research bookselling and found it difficult to locate information. I was taking a big risk and wanted to be completely sure I was making the right decision. I spent countless hours surfing the internet, gathering articles, collecting resources, and consuming information. I spent more than a year writing a business plan (while still working full time). I also began acquiring books and selling them online through Amazon.com and eBay in an effort to learn about the book industry.

My research prepared me to get started, but reality provided the best education. Throughout this guide I will share my story with you—what has and hasn't worked for me and how you can follow the same course.

The Reality of Ownership
Owning a used book store is a dream of many book-loving individuals, known as "bibliophiles" in the industry. Some see it as a great option for retirement income or as a laid-back business that is easy to run. While there are many advantages, you may not realize that running a used book store requires a heck of a lot of work!

The demands of a retail store can be great and the hours overwhelming. A successful shop must keep operating hours that cater to the public. Owners don't have the luxury of closing up and going home with a headache or calling in sick (unless of course there are employees to cover the shift).

Customers expect businesses to be open during peak hours and will complain if your store isn't open when they want to be there. This includes holidays, weekends, and the day after big holidays (the day after Thanksgiving is the biggest shopping day of the year). Holidays can present a challenge with staffing since employees may also want the day off, and often the owner is stuck working on the busiest days. Of course, this is true no matter what kind of business you own.

Pricing and shelving books is time-consuming work and can be physically demanding. As the owner, you will have to manage other business demands including bills, customer phone calls, vendors, and odd requests. You will also inevitably end up with overstock, whether from books abandoned by customers or when you have too many copies of Tom Clancy paperbacks. This means that you will be hauling books around and storing them until you can donate them to charity (which is a tax write off, so it's not a total loss).

The Perks of Book Store Ownership

If you like to read, you will have an endless selection of choices and as the store owner, you get first pick of the new inventory that comes in daily from your customers. You will also have a steady flow of regular customers and should quickly get to know them by name. If you are a social person, this can be a fun part of running this kind of business.

The financial benefits are also possible, though most will tell you that you won't get rich owning a book store. But if big money is your goal, there are many ways to generate revenues in addition to used book sales. You can ramp up your cash flow by selling gifts, greeting cards, music CDs, coffee, or other products. You might also consider offering audio book rentals, selling books on the internet, or opening multiple locations. The possibilities are limitless and the overall success is in your hands.

The bottom line is that your store is your business and you can run the show any way that you want. If there is a lot of competition where you live, you will need to be at the top of your game. Your store needs to do it different or better than your competitors.

I read somewhere that it takes a full three years for a used book store to become fully established. At the time I thought that seemed outrageous, but I have found it to be true. Keep this in mind when developing your plan. Once your store is open, you should see a steady increase in sales each month for the first three years. You can accelerate the timeline by marketing the heck out of your store and developing customer loyalty from day one.

Whether you are interested in running your store as a family business or hiring help and creating a passive income business, a used book store can be a wonderful choice. Your efforts will be helped if you have a true passion for books. If you don't, the work could end up feeling like drudgery—but this is true for any business you start.

My best advice for you is to take your time planning your business. You will be surprised by how much fear is removed from the equation when you are fully prepared for what lies ahead. I will never forget the day I quit my job. I was more nervous about letting my boss down than walking away from my paycheck. I was calm with my decision because I had done my homework and felt confident that I knew what I was getting myself into. I drove home from my last day of work in corporate America feeling *elated*.

If I had to pick the most important element of your plan it would be money—make sure you have enough of it. Running out of capital is one of the leading reasons for business failure. Have a backup plan for cash, and a backup for your backup plan. Hope you never have to use it, but have it available just in case.

Every store is different. Yours could be profitable right away, but it may take time—even more time than you expect. I know one book store owner who had to take a side job to keep his business afloat during the difficult early years. I'm not exactly sure why this was necessary for him, but my guess is that he didn't have enough cash built into his overall plan.

If you're looking for an easy business, the reality is that there is no such thing. But if you are looking for a demanding and rewarding business, then owning a book store definitely fits the profile.

I hope this book saves you the countless hours of research and planning and gets you prepared for a great adventure.

Wishing you much success,

-Stephanie Chandler

Update: I began writing this book in 2004 and published it in 2006. It is now 2007 and I am updating this book with more details and some news...

After nearly four years in business, I made the difficult decision to sell Book Lovers Book Store in 2007. During the time since I opened the store, I was also developing other interests. I published several books, launched BusinessInfoGuide.com (a directory of resources for entrepreneurs), wrote for dozens of magazines, and started a publishing business: AuthorityPublishing.com. Oh, and did I mention that I also got married and had a baby? Yes, all of this happened in just four years' time.

Starting and running Book Lovers was one of the best decisions I have ever made. I loved the store dearly, but in the last year I realized that I was juggling too many balls in the air.

I stopped working in the store on a regular basis when I went through a difficult pregnancy. Fortunately, I had a fantastic staff that kept it running well. But I still had to deal with paperwork, payroll, advertising, employees calling in sick, and all of the other challenges of owning a business. Eventually, I had to make a decision about what items I could trim from my busy schedule. I chose the book store.

Even the best business plan in the world can't account for the way life steers us in different directions. The bottom line for me was realizing that I didn't want to spend my life selling other people's books; *I would rather sell my own!*

So selling the store made sense, even if it was heart-wrenching. And though I listed the business for sale and received dozens of inquiries, one of my employees, Bradley Simkins, ultimately decided to buy the business.

I was thrilled when Brad came to me and expressed his interest. Not only would the store live on, but he didn't plan to make any major changes. In a way, it felt like the store would still be in the family. I was surprised by how possessive I felt when strangers called to inquire about buying the store. It felt like I was interviewing baby sitters and none could possibly be good enough.

Brad and his wife, Audrey, took over on June 1, 2007. I do miss the customers and having access to all that reading material! More than anything, I miss my store cats. They stayed behind because it really was their home and they have good lives there.

My decision to sell doesn't change the fact that this book is loaded with my personal experiences. And the truth is that a used book store is a difficult business to sell—and I worked very hard to build my store into a viable business.

I hope that you enjoy reading this guide and if you decide to take the journey into book store ownership, I wish you all the best. May you get as much pleasure from your business as I did from mine.

-Stephanie

Sugar and Sweetie – Book Lovers Store Cats

Section 1
Mapping Out a Plan

Long before you open, you need to begin formulating a plan. Here are some questions to consider:

✓ What is your budget?
✓ How strong is the market demand in your area?
✓ Where will you be located?
✓ Who is your competition?
✓ How will you do it better than your competitors?
✓ What is your time frame for opening?
✓ Can you keep your full time job while you plan and prepare your store?

Budget Planning

As with any business, you need to make sure you have enough working capital. When developing your budget, plan to have enough to cover your business and living expenses for at least a year. It will take time to make your store profitable and the reality is that you need to be prepared for the time that it will take.

In my case, I started saving early. I spent almost a year and a half planning my book store business, and tucked money away the whole time. There are many ways to locate capital for a business. Here are some ideas:

✓ **Personal savings.** Start saving NOW! Learn to live on a budget and set aside as much money as you can.

✓ **Sell your stuff.** Garage sales, flea markets, and eBay make it easy to liquidate things you don't need anymore. Do you have big toys such as an extra car, a jet ski, or a boat? Do you have a garage full of things you don't need, such as your grandmother's china or collectible baseball cards? Decide how important it is for you to pursue your business dreams versus hanging on to all that stuff. It might be time to liquidate.

- ✓ **Downsize your life.** Do you have a huge mortgage or rent payment? Do you have a hefty cable bill and expensive hobbies? Do you golf every weekend? Start cutting back your expenses. In my case, I was living in the Silicon Valley. I had a huge mortgage payment (and a tiny home) and didn't want the added stress of trying to keep up with that lifestyle. I packed up and moved north to Sacramento, where at the time the real estate prices were just a fraction of what they were in the Bay Area. This move dramatically reduced my cost of living and made it that much easier to give up my paycheck.

- ✓ **Cash in on investments.** Stocks, bonds, and other savings plans can provide a significant source of cash. Just be careful not to bet more than you can afford to lose.

- ✓ **Money in your house.** A home equity line can provide cash while allowing you to write off the interest that you pay.

- ✓ **Credit cards.** This is a controversial option since nobody should aspire to rack up mass amounts of credit card debt. But the fact is that this kind of debt is unsecured, which means that in most cases, your personal assets (such as your home) will not be at risk.

- ✓ **Private loans.** Do you have a relative or friend who might be willing to loan you some money? Make sure to put all agreements in writing.

- ✓ **Business loans.** You can pursue a small business loan through your bank or local Small Business Administration office. Be aware that these loans are difficult to obtain and you will need to have some assets (a house) to qualify. A list of loan information and resources is available at http://businessinfoguide.com/money.htm.

Financing Plan Worksheet

Use this chart to map out all potential sources of funding. Evaluate your liquid assets by taking an inventory of all possible sources of cash that you have available to finance your venture.

Source of Funds	Amount
Personal Savings	$
Stocks	$
Liquid Assets (sports cards, figurines, old china sets, etc.)	$
Liquid Assets—Big Toys (weekend car, motorcycle, jet ski, etc.)	$
Home Equity	$
Personal Loans	$
Investor:	$
Investor:	$
Investor:	$
Business Loans	$
Credit	$
Other	$
	$
	$
Grand Total	$

Current Personal Budget Worksheet

Before you can consider obtaining financing for your business, you need to evaluate your personal financial situation. It is important to know how much money you need to make to keep up with your current lifestyle.

Start by mapping out your monthly expenses. Once you've got a handle on what you spend, look at areas where you can cut back.

Description	Amount	Description	Amount
Rent/Mortgage		Dining Out	
Utilities		Movies/Theater/Etc.	
Phone		Hobbies	
Cell Phones		Sports/Activities	
Property Taxes		Pet Care	
Cable/Satellite TV		Prescriptions	
Home Owners Insurance		Automotive Maintenance	
Health Insurance		Gasoline	
Auto Insurance		Hair Care	
Childcare		Clothing	
Tuition		Gifts	
Groceries		Kids Entertainment	
Household Supplies		Gourmet Coffee	
DSL/Internet Access		News/Magazine Subscriptions	
Health Insurance/Co-Pays		Other	
Subtotal:		**Subtotal:**	

Grand Total:

NEW Personal Budget Worksheet

After you evaluate your current budget, fill in a new budget based on how your spending will be different once you start your business. Will you save on gasoline since you no longer have to commute? Can you reduce or eliminate your dry cleaning bill? Will your budget for clothing be reduced? Can you cut back on entertainment expenses? On the flip side, some expenses may increase. If you will be giving up health insurance, you will need to alter your budget to reflect that.

Description	Amount	Description	Amount
Rent/Mortgage		Dining Out	
Utilities		Movies/Theater/Etc.	
Phone		Hobbies	
Cell Phones		Sports/Activities	
Property Taxes		Pet Care	
Cable/Satellite TV		Prescriptions	
Home Owners Insurance		Automotive Maintenance	
Health Insurance		Gasoline	
Auto Insurance		Hair Care	
Childcare		Clothing	
Tuition		Gifts	
Groceries		Kids Entertainment	
Household Supplies		Gourmet Coffee	
DSL/Internet Access		News/Magazine Subscriptions	
Health Insurance/Co-Pays		Other	
Subtotal:		Subtotal:	

Grand Total:

Startup Costs

A common misconception about used book stores is that they cost very little to start. Unfortunately, that's not quite true, though the initial startup costs can be far less than a lot of retail businesses.

Here is a rough idea of the startup costs you can expect to incur:

Initial Inventory: 10,000 - 30,000 books The more books you can start with, the better! You can always put books on the shelf face-out to fill up the space if needed.	$5,000
Shelves Prices for shelves can vary greatly. Professional book store/library shelving can cost hundreds of dollars per fixture. Save money by building shelves yourself or buying pre-cut shelves that need to be assembled. I bought all of my shelves at Wal-Mart for about $30 each! We bolted the aisle shelves together and used elbow brackets to bolt them to the wall.	$3,000
Chairs and Miscellaneous Furniture You will probably want a chair near the cash register and may also want to place a few chairs around your shop. If you plan to hold book signing events, folding or stacking chairs can come in handy. We purchased white plastic resin patio chairs for about $6.00 each. They stack easily and work great for events. We also have a coffee table and chairs that we bought at a thrift store and use as a comfortable seating area for book clubs and writer's groups to meet. We also installed a supply cabinet and shelves in our back room, along with a card table for a break area (though it's usually covered with books) and another table where miscellaneous tasks occur.	$250
Storefront Signs Depending on where your store is located, there may be regulations governing what kind of signage you can display (ask your property manager). Neon signs are quite expensive. You may need a sign directly in front of your store and another sign for a marquee. Be sure to shop around so you get the best price—and start shopping early since it can take months for these signs to be produced.	$2,500

Checkout Counter and Display Tables A professional checkout counter will set you back a bit of cash unless you can find one used. A good desk or two can also work. Be sure to leave enough space to process incoming books. We also purchased tables for displaying books around the front of the store and covered them with inexpensive table cloths.	$1,000
Office and Cleaning Supplies There will be plenty of supplies that you need to get things going and keep them running.	$200
Shelf Signs While you can purchase professional shelf labeling supplies from a library supply company, if you have a computer, you can make them yourself and save some major cash.	$50
Neon Open Sign I purchased mine at Costco. It was so much fun to turn it on for the first time!	$150
Cash Register and Calculator While some stores still operate with hand-written paper receipts, a cash register can make it much easier to portray a professional image as well as keep your books straight. I purchased one for less than $200 at Costco. A calculator is essential for checking in incoming books. Ours prints a tape so in case we get distracted, we don't lose track of where we left off.	$250
Book Display Stands and Bookends Plastic display stands are great for displaying books upright, especially in the store window and on top of shelves around the store.	$75
Phone and Answering Machine A cordless phone can be handy since you will receive lots of calls from people asking you to search for a specific book—you can take the phone with you while you look!	$75
Security Alarm Installation This is a worthwhile investment and can give you peace of mind knowing that you will be notified if anything goes wrong after hours. Unfortunately, you can also expect the occasional false alarm when a spider makes its way across a sensor. These calls aren't fun at two a.m., but it's part of being the owner!	$150

Rolling Cart You may think this isn't an essential item, but let me assure you that it is! You will be glad you have it when there are a hundred books waiting to be put away. A flat utility-style cart works just great. We have two, which come in handy on especially busy days.	$125
Plastic T-shirt Bags You can cut corners by recycling bags and boxes, but given that t-shirt bags cost less than $20 per 1,000, they seem worthwhile to us.	$20
Stereo I personally think that music adds to the ambiance of our store. We use an inexpensive all-in-one shelf unit that rotates five CDs at a time. A boom box-style radio would also work just fine.	$50
Rent This expense will vary widely depending on where you live and how much space you rent. For example, in San Francisco, retail space can cost $25+ per square foot. In Sacramento, it can cost around $1 per square foot.	$2,000
Bookmarks Inexpensive bookmarks can be printed up and cut at your local copy shop. These are part of your marketing expenses and are a great way to remind people to come back to your store. You can print on colored copy paper or upgrade to card stock.	$50
Business Cards You will give a lot of these away at the counter so be sure to have plenty on-hand.	$40
Business Licenses Every county has different requirements and fees for business licenses. Be sure to check with yours to find out what's involved. You will also need a resale license, which allows you to purchase goods at wholesale (without paying tax) and requires that you collect sales tax with each purchase. More on business licenses will be covered in upcoming sections of this book.	$100

Liability Insurance You need to have insurance coverage in the event that anyone is ever injured at your store. Your property manager may also require that you carry a certain level of coverage. Ask your auto insurance broker if he handles liability insurance or if he can recommend someone who does. You may also need to submit your business plan to get coverage. Unfortunately, coverage is not as easy to get as you might think and you may have to try several companies before you find a provider. I use The Hartford (www.thehartford.com).	$150
Bank Fees and Checks	$30
Phone Book Advertising Listings in the yellow pages are expensive, especially if you want one that stands out. And to complicate matters, most cities have multiple phone books. Be sure to call early since these books only get printed once per year and you don't want to miss the deadline—nor can you count on them to remind you. You will be charged monthly for your ads, and as much as this feels like a big expense, the phone book is one of the first places your customers will look to find you.	$150
Other Advertising I highly recommend that you budget for advertising, especially for the first six months you're in business. We'll talk more about this later on.	$300
Merchant Card Processing System This is an essential business expense. You will lose a lot of business if you don't accept credit and debit cards. Lease fees run around $30-$50 per month for the card machine and the initial setup fee is usually extra. The processor will also get a flat transaction fee (ranging from $0.15 to $0.50 per transaction) plus a small percentage. Unfortunately, this is the cost of doing business.	$75
Professional Services (accounting, legal) I hired a bookkeeper to handle my books and found it was worth every penny. Even if you decide to do it yourself, it's a good idea to pay for a consultation to make sure you have everything in order.	$300

Miscellaneous Expenses No matter how carefully you plan, there will be unexpected expenses. Be sure to pad your budget for these.	$1,000
Total	**$17,090**
Other Items to Consider	
Refrigerator This may not be a necessity, but it sure is nice to have—especially when you start spending long hours at the store. Purchase a used one or a small dorm-sized box. A freezer can also come in handy if you start eating meals at the store regularly (TV dinners!).	$150
Microwave This is another item that is not a necessity, but can come in handy.	$70
Paper Cutter This is useful for cutting bookmarks, small flyers, etc.	$10
Renovations Depending on the space you rent or buy, you may need to make some improvements. Improvements could be as simple as a couple of coats of paint, or installing flooring and tearing down/putting up walls. You can try to get the property owner to pitch in, but many won't offer much toward improvements.	$100-$5,000
White Board We have a white board on an easel at the front of the store and use it to announce special events, new products, and special sales.	$200

This list assumes that you have your own computer and that you are doing some thrifty shopping. There is nothing wrong with acquiring furniture for your store from thrift and secondhand stores. Many large cities also have a used retail fixtures store—be sure to find one near you and check out their prices.

If this budget surprises you or seems out of range for you, get creative. Do you have access to free or low-cost shelving? Do you already have a substantial inventory of books ready to go? Do you have connections for locating some of these items at a lower cost? Can you acquire these items over time?

The important point here is that you need to do your own research and determine what your realistic budget will be. Remember, these are your startup costs—the costs you'll incur before you even turn on that open sign. You will have ongoing monthly expenses, too, and need to budget for these. The good news is that used book stores don't typically have a lot of vendors to deal with or bills for inventory since most of your inventory should start coming in on trade-in from your customers. So your monthly expenses will be relatively predictable.

Here is a sample budget of monthly expenses:

Rent (includes CAM charges)	$2,000
Utilities	$ 300
Phone and Internet Service (DSL)	$ 100
Phone Book Ads	$ 150
Other Advertising	$ 300
Liability Insurance	$ 150
Alarm Company Fee	$ 40
Office and Cleaning Supplies	$ 50
Accounting Fees	$ 100
Merchant Card Lease Fee	$ 35
Association Memberships	$ 20
Total:	**$3,245**

Suggested Shopping List for Supplies

- ✓ Pencils
- ✓ Pink Erasers
- ✓ Ballpoint Pens
- ✓ Cash Register Receipt Rolls
- ✓ Calculator Rolls
- ✓ T-shirt Bags
- ✓ Post-it Notes
- ✓ Index Cards
- ✓ Index Card File
- ✓ Envelopes
- ✓ File Folders
- ✓ File Crate or Cabinet
- ✓ Paper Clips
- ✓ Rubber Bands
- ✓ Scotch Tape
- ✓ Printer Ink Cartridges
- ✓ Scissors
- ✓ Windex
- ✓ Paper Towels
- ✓ Dust Rags
- ✓ Broom
- ✓ Mop
- ✓ Vacuum
- ✓ Price Stickers (removable so they don't damage books or other merchandise)
- ✓ Address Labels or Rubber Stamp
- ✓ Rubber Stamp for Depositing Checks
- ✓ Packing Tape (for shipping or reinforcing boxes)
- ✓ Disposable Swiffer Dusters (these are great!)
- ✓ Bathroom Cleaning Supplies
- ✓ Manual Floor Sweeper (for spot cleanups and for use while the store is open)
- ✓ Goo Gone (works great for removing price sticker glue from book covers)

Startup Supplies Worksheet

Use this worksheet to budget and track the costs of the supplies you need.

Description	Quantity	Budget Amount	Actual Spent	Variance
Totals:				

Cash Flow Forecast Worksheet

Use this worksheet to develop your cash flow forecast/performance report. If you have a spreadsheet program such as Microsoft Excel, use it to re-create this worksheet for the first two to three years. You can also purchase a pre-formatted Excel template from: www.businessinfoguide.com/products.htm

Revenue (cash in)	January	February	March	April
In-Store Sales				
Internet Sales				
Total Revenue				
Cost of Goods (cash out)				
Inventory Costs				
Other				
Total Cost of Goods				
Expenses (cash out)				
Accounting Fees				
Advertising				
Supplies				
Bank Fees				
Insurance				
Loan Interest				
Office Supplies				
Payroll				
Postage and Delivery				
Rent				
Security				
Telephone				
Utilities				
Other Expenses				
Total Expenses				
Final Calculations				
Opening Balance (cash in bank)				
Plus Revenues				
Less Cost of Goods				
Less Expenses				
Ending Cash Balance				

Revenues				
Less Cost of Goods				
Less Expenses				
Monthly Income or Loss				
Net Income or Loss				

Evaluating Market Need and Competition

How many used book stores are in your area? Are there five, ten, or twenty stores? Large towns can support multiple stores in different neighborhoods, but small towns can probably only handle a few stores—unless you specialize in an especially popular genre.

If there is a lot of competition in your area, you will need to find a way to set your business apart. Start by identifying the advantages of each store and then how you can compete. Here are some ways to stand out in a crowded market:

- ✓ Offer better prices
- ✓ Be more organized/neater than the others
- ✓ Offer coffee, tea, or snacks
- ✓ Specialize in certain genres (mysteries, sci-fi, and collectibles are popular)
- ✓ Have longer hours of operation
- ✓ Sell other items such as gifts, greeting cards, music, audio books, large print books, and homeschool books
- ✓ Provide audio book rentals
- ✓ Offer special orders of new or out-of-print books
- ✓ Sell gift certificates
- ✓ Sell used music CDs or other rare used goods
- ✓ Host events featuring local authors, writers, or musicians

Evaluate your closest competitors to make sure you have a plan of action. Use the following form to evaluate at least three of your competitors. If you don't have any competition in your immediate area, then be sure to evaluate stores outside of your area to get ideas.

Competitor Evaluation Worksheet

Competitor Name	
Approximate Size of Store	
Location	
Hours of Operation	
Products and Services Offered	
Key Features (cleanliness, friendliness, selection, etc.)	
Pricing Structure (half of list price? More? Less?)	
Coupons, discounts, or frequent buyer programs?	
Book trade policy (what kinds of books do they accept? Do they pay cash or issue credit only? How much credit/cash is issued? How liberal is their policy?)	
Do they advertise? Where? How?	
Inventory Selection (do they specialize in any special genres? Any genres missing from their stock?)	
Overall Appearance of Store (neat, messy, run-down?)	
Do they have a website? What kind of information does it include?	
Other Notes:	

Location, Location, Location

Location is an issue for many businesses, and book stores are no exception. When I opened Book Lovers, I settled on a rather inconvenient location in a shopping center that doesn't generate a lot of foot traffic. Here's your chance to learn from my mistakes! What I saved in rent I had to spend on advertising to make up for it. If you can locate your store in a shopping center with an anchor store (a large supermarket or department store), you will be more likely to get foot traffic from day one. Of course, these locations are more expensive so you have to calculate the numbers in your business plan and make sure it will work for you.

Used book stores are primarily a neighborhood destination. Your main customer base will come from a five- or ten-mile radius so it's important to be located in a densely populated neighborhood. If your store is special enough or you're the only used book store for miles, you could draw customers from other cities, but your loyal, regular customers are going to live in the neighborhood and become the bread and butter of your store.

If the rents aren't reasonable in the big shopping centers near you, then look to smaller strip malls. Ideally you want to be located near a complementary business or one that generates lots of local traffic, such as a coffee shop. Make sure to evaluate the street visibility, access to parking, and how easy it will be for customers to get to you.

Areas with higher than average income levels are worth considering since the residents are likely to be educated and therefore, readers. Colleges, schools, and retirement communities can also bring readers your way.

Commercial Leases
When it comes to leasing space, I strongly suggest enlisting some professional help. Too many business owners take this on themselves and end up frustrated in the process. While there are "For Lease" signs posted on buildings across America with phone numbers that make it easy to simply dial from your cell phone when you drive by, this is not the best way to go. Find a commercial Realtor—a good one that you like and respect—and have her assist you in finding a space and negotiating your lease.

Without your own representation, you will deal with the Realtor or property manager that represents the property owner and you will have to look out for your own best interests. If you have a strong personality or a sales background, this may not seem like a major obstacle, but you will be dealing with all new terminology, conditions, and contracts you have never encountered before.

Your Realtor shouldn't charge you a fee. Her fees should be paid by the property owner upon closing so it will cost you nothing to have the benefit of her expertise. A good Realtor has the advantage of experience and can tell you the pros and cons of different neighborhoods and buildings. While you should ultimately decide what you are willing to negotiate, a professional Realtor will handle the negotiations and will help you review the contract details.

Also be prepared to view a lot of properties before you make your decision. Many business owners will tell you that it takes time to find the right location that meets the needs of your business and your budget. Viewing a lot of properties will also help you compare and contrast your options. But try not to get too emotionally attached to a property. This could cause you to agree to terms that you wouldn't otherwise want to accept—such as a lease that is longer in duration than you want or rent that is higher than your budget calls for.

Location Assessment Worksheet—Part One

Use this worksheet to assess each location that you see. After you look at several different properties, the features will begin to run together. This worksheet will help make your evaluation process easier.

Name of Building/Shopping Center:	
Address:	
Cross Street:	
Anchor Store/Nearby Businesses:	
Utilities Included?	
Average Operating Hours of Neighboring Businesses:	
Security?	
Parking Availability, Cost, and Proximity:	
Proximity to Competition:	
Storage Area Size and Description:	
Kitchen Area Detail:	
Bathroom Area Detail:	
Back Office Area Detail:	
General Description of Property:	
Color and Condition of Flooring:	
Any Fixtures Included?	
Repairs/Improvements Needed?	

Location Assessment Worksheet—Part Two

Freeway Access?		**Public Transit Access?**	
Square Footage:		**Foot Traffic?**	
Price:		**NNN/CAM Charges?**	
Street Visibility?		**Marquee Signage?**	
Central Heat?		**Central A/C?**	
Age of Roof:		**Building Last Painted:**	

Additional Questions to Ask:

Notes:

Section 2
Business Basics: What You Need To Start a Business

Business License

Every state, city, and county has different regulations for general business licenses. The fees range from $50 to $300 and are renewed each year.

Certain types of businesses may also be required to apply for special business licenses, and used book stores can fall into this category. Since you will be selling used goods, your county could lump you together with thrift and antique stores and require you to obtain an additional special permit. These licenses can also take longer to be issued, sometimes up to three months, so be sure to apply early. Contact your local offices to find out the requirements for your store.

Business License Resources by State
- ✓ Alabama - www.ador.state.al.us/licenses/authrity.html
- ✓ Alaska - www.dced.state.ak.us/occ/buslic.htm
- ✓ Arizona - www.revenue.state.az.us/license.htm
- ✓ Arkansas - www.state.ar.us/online_business.php
- ✓ California - www.calgold.ca.gov/
- ✓ Colorado - www.state.co.us/gov_dir/obd/blid.htm
- ✓ Connecticut - www.state.ct.us/
- ✓ Delaware - www.state.de.us/revenue/obt/obtmain.htm
- ✓ District of Columbia - www.dcra.dc.gov/
- ✓ Florida - http://sun6.dms.state.fl.us/dor/businesses/
- ✓ Georgia - www.sos.state.ga.us/corporations/regforms.htm
- ✓ Hawaii - www.hawaii.gov/dbedt/start/starting.html
- ✓ Idaho - www.idoc.state.id.us/Pages/BUSINESSPAGE.html
- ✓ Illinois - www.sos.state.il.us/departments/business_services/business.html
- ✓ Indiana - www.state.in.us/sic/owners/ia.html
- ✓ Iowa - www.iowasmart.com/blic/
- ✓ Kansas - www.accesskansas.org/businesscenter/index.html?link=start
- ✓ Kentucky - www.thinkkentucky.com/kyedc/ebpermits.asp

- ✓ Louisiana - www.sec.state.la.us/comm/fss/fss-index.htm
- ✓ Maine - www.econdevmaine.com/biz-develop.htm
- ✓ Maryland - www.dllr.state.md.us/
- ✓ Massachusetts - www.state.ma.us/sec/cor/coridx.htm
- ✓ Michigan - http://medc.michigan.org/services/startups/index2.asp
- ✓ Minnesota - www.dted.state.mn.uss
- ✓ Mississippi - www.olemiss.edu/depts/mssbdc/going_intobus.html
- ✓ Missouri - www.ded.state.mo.us/business/businesscenter/
- ✓ Montana - www.state.mt.us/sos/biz.htm
- ✓ Nebraska - www.nebraska.gov/business/html/337/index.phtml
- ✓ New Hampshire - www.nhsbdc.org/startup.htm
- ✓ New Jersey - www.state.nj.us/njbiz/s_lic_and_cert.shtml
- ✓ New York - www.dos.state.ny.us/lcns/licensing.html
- ✓ New Mexico - http://edd.state.nm.us/NMBUSINESS/
- ✓ Nevada - www.nv.gov
- ✓ North Carolina - www.secstate.state.nc.us/secstate/blio/default.htm
- ✓ North Dakota - www.state.nd.us/sec/
- ✓ Ohio - www.state.oh.us/sos/business_services_information.htm
- ✓ Oklahoma - www.okonestop.com/
- ✓ Oregon - www.filinginoregon.com
- ✓ Pennsylvania - www.paopenforbusiness.state.pa.us
- ✓ Rhode Island - www.corps.state.ri.us/firststop/index.asp
- ✓ South Carolina - www.state.sd.us/STATE/sitecategory.cfm?mp=Licenses/Occupations
- ✓ South Dakota - www.sd.gov/Main_Login.asp
- ✓ Tennessee - www.state.tn.us/ecd/res_guide.htm
- ✓ Texas - www.tded.state.tx.us/guide/
- ✓ Utah - www.commerce.state.ut.us/web/commerce/admin/licen.htm
- ✓ Vermont - www.sec.state.vt.us/
- ✓ Virginia - www.dba.state.va.us/licenses/
- ✓ Washington - www.wa.gov/dol/bpd/limsnet.htm
- ✓ West Virginia - www.state.wv.us/taxrev/busreg.html
- ✓ Wisconsin - www.wdfi.org/corporations/forms/
- ✓ Wyoming - http://soswy.state.wy.us/corporat/corporat.htm

Additional Resources:
- ✓ The IRS also offers links to every state with multiple business resources: www.irs.gov/businesses/small/article/0,,id=99021,00.html

✓ Business.gov provides legal and regulatory information to small businesses in the U.S. This site is loaded with excellent information for every state to help entrepreneurs find answers and resolve problems and can be found at: www.Business.gov.

Federal Tax ID

A federal tax ID, also known as an Employer Identification Number (EIN), is used for tax reporting purposes. You need a federal tax ID number if you have one or more employees on a payroll or if you form a corporation. Sole proprietors without employees can usually use their social security number for tax reporting and are not required to apply for a federal ID (though you can still apply for one if you don't want to use your Social Security number). Visit www.irs.gov/businesses/small/article/0,,id=98350,00.html for more information or to apply using form SS-4.

Resale Certificate

A resale license is necessary for any business that sells taxable goods. This license also allows you to purchase books and other products from wholesalers without paying sales tax, which also means that you are responsible for collecting taxes when you make a sale. Each state and local authority has different requirements for tax rates, collection, and reporting methods. The Business Owner's Tool Kit website has an excellent directory of tax requirements for each state: www.toolkit.cch.com/text/P07_4500.asp.

Insurance

Liability Insurance
Liability insurance protects you from lawsuits or liabilities filed by customers or employees. If a customer slips and falls in your place of business, your insurance policy should cover the damages. If you are ever the target of a frivolous lawsuit, your insurance policy should take care of the legal fees and litigations. Not all policies are created equal, however, so be sure to check the details of any policy that you consider.

If you are going to lease a commercial location for your business, your landlord will probably require proof of liability insurance. Since the fees for this type of insurance can vary, it is a good idea to get some quotes early on and build this expense into your budget.

Property Coverage

In the event of a disaster (for example, if a water pipe breaks and floods your building) or other property damage, property coverage can protect you from losses. Fixed property insurance should cover the building itself and can also cover the contents such as fixtures and inventory. If you are renting the building, the property owner probably carries some level of insurance. You should ask what is covered in his policy. When in doubt, it is always best to carry your own policy.

Workers' Compensation Insurance

Many states now require that companies with employees carry workers' compensation insurance. This type of policy covers damages resulting from employee injuries. It is relatively expensive in some states (like California) so it would be wise to factor this into your plan early. Check the state listings provided in this chapter to find out if your area requires that you carry workers' comp insurance.

Where to Locate Insurance Providers

Contact the broker that handles your auto or home owner's insurance to find out if he also offers business insurance. If not, he should be able to refer you to someone who does. You can also visit www.InsuranceFinder.com for a list of resources by state.

The Business Plan

You will need a business plan if you plan to apply for a business loan. Even if you aren't seeking funding, the process of writing a business plan is an excellent way to educate and prepare yourself for running your business. Committing your plan to paper helps you anticipate many aspects of running your business and can cause you to consider topics you hadn't already considered.

Business plans can be short and sweet, or very detailed (between 5 and 100 pages). If you are seeking a loan, you plan should also educate the lender about the bookselling industry and demonstrate that you are fully prepared to run the business.

I have included the actual business plan I developed for Book Lovers in the appendix of this book. The following is a basic outline, which you can use as a general guideline. You don't have to stick to it exactly and should modify it to suit your needs and style.

Business Plan Outline

I. Company Description/Overview

    A. Nature of Business

        1. Individuals being served/their needs
        2. Why your area?

    B. Your Distinctive Competencies (primary factors that will lead to your success)

        1. Superior customer need satisfaction
        2. Production/service delivery efficiencies
        3. Personnel
        4. Geographic location

II. Market Analysis

    A. Target Markets

        1. Demographics
        2. Geographic location
        3. Seasonal/cyclical trends

    B. Competition

        1. Identification
        2. Strengths (competitive advantages)
        3. Weaknesses (competitive disadvantages)

III. Products and Services

    A. Detailed Product/Service Description (from the user's perspective)

        1. Specific benefits of product/service
        2. Ability to meet needs
        3. Competitive advantages

IV. Marketing and Sales Activities

    A. Overall Market Strategy

        1. Market penetration strategy
          a. Intended means (including advertising, promotion, printed matter, etc.)

        2. Growth Strategy

V. Management and Ownership

    A. Management Staff Structure
    B. Key Managers (including self)

        1. Name
        2. Position
        3. Primary responsibilities and authority
        4. Primary responsibilities and authority with previous employers
        5. Unique skills and experiences that add to your company's distinctive competencies

    C. Legal Structure of the Business

VI. Organization and Personnel

    A. Recruitment procedures
    B. Staffing levels

*****

Logo and Business Identity

Having a logo is not an absolute necessity for your business, but it certainly adds a level of professionalism and personality to your store. You can hire a graphics designer to develop yours for you. The cost for this service ranges from $250 - $500. Freelance designers can be found at www.elance.com or www.allfreelancework.com.

If you have an eye for design and want to take a stab at designing a logo yourself, you can use any number of graphic design programs or an inexpensive solution such as LogoWorks, offered by Laughing Bird Software (www.laughingbird.com).

If an official logo is not high on your priority list, you can get by with some clip art from Microsoft or any graphics program. Just try to be consistent with the images that you use so you can begin to form a recognizable business identity.

Logo for Book Lovers Book Store

Section 3
Learning about Bookselling

What Makes a Book Collectible?

I am asked this question often and there are a few reasons that a book can be categorized as collectible. The most obvious collectibles are the first editions of books that later achieved greatness or by authors who went on to become literary or cult icons. A true first edition of Stephen King's first book, *Christine*, or J.K. Rowling's *Harry Potter* are worth thousands of dollars.

Some people like to collect first editions by their favorite authors. I have customers who collect Tom Clancy and Dean Koontz, even though the subsequent first editions don't retain much value.

Books that are signed by the author can also increase in value, but only if the author is in high demand and hasn't signed a lot of books. Of course, anything signed by classic authors like Mark Twain or J.D. Salinger are in a valuable class all their own.

Books that were printed in small runs and later became cult classics can also increase in value over time. These are usually books with unusual subject matter. The very first collectible book I sold was a ratty old paperback about Los Angeles pimps! That book sold for an astonishing $70 online! The moral of this story is that you should look up any unusual books to see if the value has increased.

Identifying Collectibles

Identifying first editions is an art in itself. Some of the big publishers make it easier by stating "First Edition" on the copyright page, but that doesn't always mean that the book is a true first edition. The first place to check is the number line on the copyright page. A true first edition should look something like this:

1 2 3 4 5 6 7 8 9 10

Number lines that start with a "1" *usually* indicate a first printing. The print run is typically the lowest number in the chain. For example:

6 7 8 9 10 11 12 13 14 15

The number above indicates that the book is a sixth edition or printing.

Since not all publishers conform to these standards, especially in decades past, you may have to do some additional homework to verify the print run of the book in question. The copyright date can help. If you see a date that is later than the original print date for the book, then you can be certain you don't have a first edition.

When you have a signed copy, you may want to verify that the signature is authentic. Unless you are an expert with years of experience, you will need to find a creative way to do this. I personally long onto eBay and look for other items signed by the author in question. Most sellers include a picture of the signature and you can compare multiple pictures with the signature in your book. It's not an exact science, but it can help. I once had a signature in a book that was clearly a fake once I looked at the different pictures on eBay and saw a clear signature pattern by that author.

There are some great books that describe the intricacies of collectible books, publishers, and how to identify collectibles. Check out these titles:
- ✓ *Instant Expert – Book Collecting* by Matthew Budman
- ✓ *Book Finds – How to Find, Buy and Sell Used and Rare Books* by Ian Ellis

Book Valuation

The price of a collectible book depends greatly on the condition. In the bookselling industry, there are terms that most book dealers use universally. When identifying the condition of a book, most dealers use a rating system of "fine," "near fine," "good," "fair," or "poor." A book in fine condition can be worth significantly more, sometimes by hundreds or thousands of dollars, than one that is in poor condition.

A book that is in fine condition is a rare find in itself. Fine condition means that there are no noticeable flaws, no rubbing from shelf wear, pages are clean and unmarked—the book essentially looks new.

A book in near fine condition has a few flaws—perhaps a scratch or two to the dust jacket or cover, the previous owner's name might be on the first page, or it has a few minor flaws. The book should still look nearly new if it is going to be rated as near fine.

A book that is in good condition has some noticeable flaws, but nothing that degrades the overall quality of the book. For example, the book may have some shelf wear on the dust jacket or the book looks like it has been read a few times.

A book that is in fair condition has some serious flaws. The dust jacket may be torn or missing, the binding may be coming loose, there could be water damage or any number of factors that cause you to look at the book and think that it has seen some better days.

A book in poor condition would probably be destined for the trash bin. The cover has come loose, pages are loose, the cover is heavily damaged, and other major flaws are obvious. Many book dealers won't even sell a book in this condition.

Resources for Price Guidelines

Thanks to the internet, determining book prices has become much easier. I search the online book sites to check the prices and conditions of the same title listed for sale by other book dealers. This is a great way to determine the market demand and set your price at a comparable level.

Check out www.abe.com or www.bookfinder.com to research book values.

Section 4
Locating Suppliers

Finding suppliers was one of the most frustrating tasks I faced when I started, but I'm here to make this a lot easier for you.

Library and Archival Supplies

Depending on your budget, you may want to order shelf signs, plastic covers for collectible books, book display stands, archival supplies, or even fancy display cases. All of these are available through library supply companies. You can contact all of them and sign up to have a catalog mailed to you at any time. The three most popular library supply companies are
- ✓ Brodart: www.shopbrodart.com/
- ✓ Vernon: www.vernonlibrarysupplies.com/
- ✓ Gaylord: www.gaylord.com/

In my own experience, prices can vary widely for various items from each of these suppliers. Be sure to compare before you buy and take advantage of sale offers. It's also a good idea to sign up for the e-mail newsletter since they frequently send special promotional offers.

Shelves
If you have the labor and resources, you can build your shelves with inexpensive lumber. I would suggest you stain or paint them to keep them looking sharp. Make sure you mount them either to the floor, ceiling, or walls to meet fire and safety codes.

Office Supplies

Office supplies can be delivered by most companies if you meet the minimum order requirements—usually $50. Be sure to sign up for the mailing lists to receive special sales and coupons. The big stores also have special shopping programs for businesses that will give you additional discounts and even cash

back on your purchases, so be sure to sign up for these. Here are the biggest stores:
- ✓ Office Depot: www.officedepot.com/
- ✓ Staples: www.staples.com/
- ✓ Office Max: www.officemax.com/

Bookmarks

You will want to print bookmarks to include with each sale. Bookmarks are an inexpensive way to advertise your business and remind your customers to come back. While you can spend a hefty sum on having these designed and printed at a professional print shop, your best bet is to design them yourself and have them copied and professionally cut at your local office supply or copy store.

Bookmarks and other templates are available for free on Microsoft's website: http://office.microsoft.com/en-us/templates/default.aspx

When designing your bookmarks, be sure to include your logo, store name, location, phone number, and website URL (if you have one). You may also want to include your store hours and use the rest of the space to advertise some of the items your store sells. Avoid printing your store hours, however, if there is a chance they are going to change, so you don't waste money on printing.

Color printing will cost you up to ten times as much as printing in black ink. To stick to your budget, print your bookmarks with black ink on colored paper. Most copy shops will print on pastel paper for the same price as white paper. If you can afford a few extra dollars, print your bookmarks on slightly heavier bond paper. Standard copy paper has a 20 lb weight, but the 65 lb weight paper makes a nice, sturdy bookmark that could be used by your customer for months or even years. Your local print shop or office supply store can also cut the bookmarks for you for an extra fee, or you can use your own paper cutter and do this yourself. I find it's worth the extra pennies to let them do this for me.

Be careful not to print too many bookmarks with your first run since you will probably decide to change the text on your bookmarks as time goes by or your store hours change.

Business Cards, Labels, and Rubber Stamps

There are countless companies that offer affordable options for business cards, labels, and rubber stamps. You may want to visit your local office supply or printing store. Two of my favorite online resources for printed supplies are www.VistaPrint.com and www.iPrint.com. Be sure to sign up for their mailing lists since both have fantastic sales on their services each week.

I personally decided to purchase pre-cut shelves that simply needed to be assembled. You can buy the wood grain or white laminate shelves from discount stores like Wal-Mart (where I got mine) or K-Mart for around $30 per shelf. I like them because the shelves are adjustable. However, you could save some space by building thinner shelves for paperbacks. The pre-cut shelves do take up more space than needed, but they look nice.

Shelves are one of your largest expenses and labor efforts, so consider your options carefully before deciding on the right choice for you. If you have a great budget, you can purchase professional shelving from the library supply stores or investigate options from your local secondhand retail supply shop.

Retail Supplies

I order my t-shirt bags, video cameras, and other supplies from Valu Display (www.valudisplay.com) and Specialty Store Services (www.specialtystoreservices.com). If you prefer to shop locally, check your phone book for retail fixtures or retail supplies.

Greeting Cards and Gift Items

If you decide to carry items other than books, greeting cards may be a good option. I would suggest carrying unique or unusual cards that customers can't find in very many places. In my store, I carry funny cards by Portal and I have customers who come in just to buy cards. I started with a single rack of cards when I opened and now have three racks. These sell well and add to the overall ambiance of the store.

I also carry boxed cards and puzzles from Leanin' Tree. Here are some popular card suppliers to consider:

- ✓ Blue Mountain: www.bluemountain.com/index_homec.pd
- ✓ Portal Cards: www.portalpub.com/
- ✓ Leanin' Tree: www.leanintree.com/

I am always on the lookout for unique products when I travel or visit an interesting boutique. If you find a product you like at another gift shop, purchase one and then get in touch with the vendor on the label.

Another great way to locate all kinds of items is to attend a gift industry trade show. These happen in major cities all over the country. Vendors display their products so you can pick up information or place orders on the spot. Check out the Trade Show Network (www.tsnn.com/) to locate a directory of gift shows in your area.

Merchant Accounts

You will need the ability to accept credit cards and it seems like everyone is peddling merchant accounts. Not a month goes by when someone doesn't try to sell me a new package. It can be very overwhelming.

You should start by checking with the bank where your business account is located. Unfortunately, the reality is that many banks won't issue these systems to new businesses. Due to the high rate of fraud and business failure, most major banks don't want to take the chance—even on their own customers. Don't take it personally.

If your bank won't help you, you will have to shop around. Most likely you will begin to receive offers from merchant systems providers as soon as you apply for a business license (they purchase mailing lists). Be sure to compare the rates of several providers before you make a decision.

Because there are so many providers, I hesitate to make any recommendations for merchant services. My advice is to ask for *written quotes* from several providers. You can also ask business associates or your chamber of commerce to recommend providers. Transaction rates and equipment lease terms can vary greatly so written quotes will allow you to find the best deal in your area.

Section 5
Acquiring Inventory

There is no doubt that acquiring good used books will be the most time-consuming task and probably one of the greatest challenges you will face. The most obvious venues are thrift stores and garage sales, though there are plenty of other options.

Before you go looking, decide what you are willing to pay and what quality you are willing to accept. I sell books at half their retail value; therefore, I won't pay more than twenty-five percent of a book's cover price, unless it happens to be a hot item or bestseller. However, when you are buying in large quantities and working within a budget, you should set a goal of buying books as cheaply as possible. You may be able to find thrift stores that sell paperbacks as low as $0.25-$0.50 each and hardcovers for $1.00-$2.00.

Use some negotiating skills at garage sales and flea markets. If the sellers have a large box of books priced individually, offer a flat price for the entire box. These people are likely to want to just get rid of them and will be happy to have less to clean up when the sale is over. I was once at a garage sale where the owner had a giant box of books marked for $2.00 each. I offered him $20 for the whole box (about 80 books) and he was thrilled.

Don't forget to save every receipt when you buy books and write down your mileage in a pocket calendar. Both are expenses that you can write off at tax time. If you buy from personal parties, bring your own receipt book so you always have a record of everything you spend.

The following are additional places to find your inventory:

Library Book Sales

Just about every library has an occasional sale to liquidate books that have been donated along with books taken out of library circulation. Some libraries even sponsor a special room of books for sale where you can find some great bargains any day of the week. I have found several libraries that sell books for $0.25 each.

Even if you can't find the most popular titles, you will certainly find some books in good condition that will help fill your shelves.

Join your local Friends of the Library and get on the mailing list so you will be notified of special sales in your area. Many libraries have a special preview day for members, which will allow you to have the chance to buy a day before the public arrives. You will be elbow-to-elbow with plenty of book dealers and scouts, so be prepared to deal with these crowds. Book scouts can be ruthless! To locate library sales in your area, visit: www.booksalefinder.com/. Make sure to sign up for their mailing list, which will notify you of sales in your area each week.

Classified Ads

Classified ads in the "Wanted" section are a great way to find people with large quantities of books to sell. The key here is not to waste your time on anyone with less than 50 books; otherwise, you'll run around town for days picking up small stacks of books. Set expectations in your ad so you don't get lots of calls from people trying to get rich by selling their ratty paperbacks. Try an ad similar to this one:

Wanted to Buy: Large quantities of used books (100 or more, please). Must be in good condition. Will pay $0.50/paperback and $1.50/hardback.

If you think that people won't be willing to part with books for such a small fee, you're in for a surprise. Some people are thrilled to unload their books. Some may have inherited a collection from a relative or simply have books overrunning their house. The idea of making a few bucks off the sale and clearing out the space can be very appealing.

When you get calls—and you will—get as many details as possible. Have the books been in storage? If they have been boxed up nicely, this shouldn't be a problem. But some basements can leave books with a musty odor or even with water damage. Make sure it's clear that you only want books in excellent condition.

If you aren't comfortable going to people's homes, offer to meet in a public place such as a parking lot in a local shopping center. Make sure to make up a receipt (even though you are the one doing the buying, you shouldn't expect the general public to do this for you) so you can keep track of your purchases come tax time.

Post ads in your local newspapers. You can also post free classified ads online at www.craigslist.org.

Store Overstock

Contact used book stores *out of your area* and ask about buying their overstock. Every used book store has overstock (you will, too). Each store has a different policy, but most likely the overstock will come from books that are in abundance and that the store simply doesn't have room for. As a result, many donate their overstock to charities for a tax write-off.

The key with this option is to contact a store at least 30 miles away from you. Your local competition isn't going to be eager to help you. Contact the owners and explain that you are opening a store in XYZ city and want to inquire about buying some of their overstock. Most stores will jump on this opportunity to get rid of their overflow for quick cash instead of waiting for that tax break. You should be able to negotiate a bargain price. Strike up a rapport with the owner. Remember, they have been in your shoes and may want to help you by making you a great offer.

Also don't expect the latest and greatest titles. Overstock is the stuff that has been weeded out and will primarily end up being space filler for your store. Some of the biggest authors have had their books printed in the millions and every used book store is overloaded with them (for example, Tom Clancy, John Grisham, and Danielle Steele).

Going Out of Business Sale

Even if you don't want to buy an existing book store, you may be able to acquire inventory from one that is closing. If the business hasn't found a buyer, or the owner just wants out quickly, you could strike a great deal and have an entire store inventory ready to go.

The bulk of inventory for my store in California came from a store in Florida. We found each other through the internet. I had a classified ad out for "Books Wanted" and the owner of the Florida store that was closing sent me an e-mail. We spoke on the phone several times until I felt confident this was a good deal. I did a lot of comparison shopping to locate the most inexpensive shipper. A month later I had 23,000 books shipped across the U.S. In fact, the weight of the books actually broke the axle on the truck that delivered them! The books were put straight into a storage unit until I was ready to open my shop.

To locate book stores for sale, you can start by checking on eBay. You can also surf the internet for "book store for sale." Even if the store is hundreds of miles away, you may be able to strike a deal with the owner that makes it worth the price of shipping to fill your store from day one.

There are many databases of businesses for sale on the internet. Here are some to get you started:
- ✓ www.bizbuysell.com/
- ✓ www.bizquest.com/buy/
- ✓ www.thebusinessmarket.com/

Family and Friends

Tell everyone you know. You might be surprised by how your friends and family are thrilled to have a reason to clear out their bookshelves. Once I got the word out that I was opening a store, my friends and family started bringing me books by the trunk-load. They seemed to like that they could help me out while clearing out some space at home. I never even asked for their help—but when I told them I was starting a used book store, they all chipped in and continue to do so today. Your family and friends will probably be thrilled to help you.

Book Drives

Schools, churches, and charitable organizations are always looking for new ways to hold fundraising events. You can offer to sponsor a book drive for any of these organizations. The way to set it up is to have the organization alert their members, letting them know to bring their books to a specified drop-off location (usually at the organization's headquarters). You indicate a period of time in which the book drive will last, perhaps 30 days or so, and agree to pay them for each book collected. You could again offer something like $0.50 per paperback and $1.50 or $2.00 per hardback. Make sure to set a maximum amount you are willing to pay so you don't end up spending thousands of dollars when you only budgeted for a few hundred.

It would be best if you already have your business license and business name established to offer credibility while promoting your business. I ran several of these shortly after opening my store as a way to fill up the shelves quickly. The organizations are thrilled because it's a low-effort event on their part. When the book drive is over, have them bring the books to you or offer to pick them up.

To locate organizations interested in participating in book drives, you can put together a flier or letter and send them to all of the schools, churches, and non-profits in your area. You could also get out the phone book and start making calls. The following is a sample agreement similar to the one I use to host these events:

Book Drive Agreement

Book Lovers Book Store agrees to sponsor a Book Drive under the terms of this agreement with _____ (organization). The organization agrees to run the Book Drive between the dates of _____ and _____. Upon completion, the organization will deliver the collected books to Book Lovers no later than _____(date).

Book Lovers agrees to pay $1.50 per hardback and $0.50 per paperback or children's book up to a maximum of $500.00. Books must be in good used condition without excessive wear. Bindings and pages must be intact, books must be clean, and hardbacks should have dust jackets. Hardbacks without dust jackets will be paid at the paperback rate. Magazines and other paper products do not qualify for payment. Books may be from any genre including fiction, non-fiction, and children's books.

Book Lovers will pay the organization upon delivery of the books to the Book Lovers store location at 5800 Madison Avenue, Sacramento. Books should be delivered in bags or boxes along with a count of total hardbacks and paperbacks.

The organization agrees to advertise the Book Drive and Book Lovers as its sponsor. The books may be used in Book Lovers inventory; however, many may also be donated to another charitable organization.

*Book Lovers Authorization*_____   *Date:*_____

*Organization Authorization*_____   *Date:*_____

Storage Auctions

Storage facilities regularly hold auctions to sell off the contents of storage units that have been abandoned by renters. The contents of the units are auctioned off as-is, and buyers must take all of the contents as part of the sale. The entire unit contents typically sell for $5-$500, depending on what kind of treasures are inside. Salvage dealers attend these sales, buying the merchandise on the cheap and reselling for a profit.

Books are not an item that most salvage dealers want, and when they are found inside these units, they often end up in the trash. If you don't want to buy an entire unit, your best bet may be to network with the people attending the auctions. Most of attendees make a career in the salvage industry and may be thrilled to have a contact to call when they come across books. They will be willing to sell you large quantities of books for pennies on the dollar because it will be one less thing they have to dump. Plus, you'll be saving a lot of wonderful books from an untimely death at the dump. Call your local storage facilities for auction dates and times.

Thrift Store Auctions

Like the auctions held at storage facilities, large thrift store chains (including the Salvation Army and Goodwill) also hold auctions at their main distribution centers. Books are almost always on the block and sell for incredibly low prices in bulk. Call the thrift store chains in your area to inquire.

Independent Thrift Stores

Books are not typically a top-seller for thrift stores since most of these businesses focus on higher-ticket items. You can contact thrift store owners and offer to buy their overstock of books (most receive more than they can handle). This strategy worked quite well for me when I opened. The smaller, independent stores are much easier to deal with and more likely to want to work with you than the larger stores.

Consignment

If you plan to deal in collectibles or need to fill up a certain genre in your store, you could offer to sell books on consignment. To set this up, contact some of the specialty book dealers in your area—especially those who only deal online and do not have their own storefront. They may have overstock or just some books that they would love to display in a different location. Write up an agreement to sell their books, keeping a margin of 30%-40% for yourself and paying the vendor after the books have sold.

This is a strategy I used for audio books and science fiction. A gentleman who writes audio book reviews contacted me and offered to sell his audio inventory on consignment at my store. Then I met a science fiction dealer who works from his home and we worked out a similar agreement. Though it equates to extra tracking and inventory procedures, it has been a great way to keep some popular sections loaded with hot titles.

Local Authors

Most communities are full of writers, and self-publishing has opened doors for unknown writers to get their words in print. Self-published authors are eager to get their books into stores any way they can, and that includes selling them on consignment. The added advantage of accepting books by local authors is that each of those authors will be promoting your store, letting people know that their books are available there.

The standard discount for book stores should be 40% off the retail price of the book. To locate authors and get the word out, contact writers' groups and publishing associations in your area. Let them know your store accepts books by local authors and they will be happy to spread the word to their members.

Use the internet to search for these groups. For example, to locate these groups in Sacramento, I would search with the following keywords:

✓ Sacramento writers
✓ Sacramento publishers
✓ Sacramento writers group
✓ Sacramento publishers association

The following is an example of the consignment agreement we use with local authors.

Book Lovers Book Store Book Consignment Agreement

Book Lovers Book Store accepts _____ copies of _____
                              Quantity   *Book Title*

from_____ on _____. The retail
          Author Name   *Date*

price of the book is $_____ and the discount to Book Lovers is _____%, with a
                     Price   *Percentage*

total cost of $_____ per book.
              Book Lovers Cost

Book Lovers Book Store accepts the books on consignment and agrees to pay author for

copies sold when the net due to the author exceeds $25 or quarterly if sales do not exceed

$25. Book Lovers takes full responsibility for the books accepted and will pay for any

shortages in inventory.

Author payments should be Payable to: _____
                                        Author or Publisher Name

And mailed to _____.
              Mailing Address for Payments

_____   _____
Book Lovers Representative & Date   Author & Date

Section 6
<u>Setting Up Shop</u>

Store Layout

Take time when designing your floor plan. It's best if you can get or make a diagram of your square footage and sketch out where your shelves will be placed and how your aisles will be configured. You could hire a professional space planner to do this for you, but be prepared to spend at least $1,000 for this service.

A software program called Visio can also be used for this purpose. If you don't have access to Visio, you can make your own chart using graph paper or just plain old paper. I measured out my store and drew different configurations until I settled on one that worked best.

Your aisles should be wide enough to allow wheelchair access, not only because the American Disabilities Act requires this, but because it will keep your store from feeling too cramped. It may be difficult to give up precious square footage, but your customers—all of them—will appreciate that it is easier to get around your store.

Your cash register should be near the front door so you can keep an eye on people coming and going. Make sure there are plenty of power outlets and a phone line in the area.

Also consider whether you're going to have display tables or other types of merchandising fixtures and factor these into your floor plans. You may also want to have a seating area if space allows and if you plan to hold any events.

Laying out your aisles will help give you an accurate estimate of how many shelves you will need. One option to consider is leaving some space to add more shelves later—after you have been open for awhile and have more books to fill them.

To create aisles, we used inexpensive pre-cut shelves and lined them up back-to-back. We then used flat brackets to bolt them together at the top, and L-brackets to bolt shelves to the walls. This is not only a good idea for safety reasons, but some earthquake-prone states are required to do this.

Once you have your layout plans, you can start to decide how your books will be organized. It's best if you can group similar genres together. The smallest sections, such as large print books, humor, and movie tie-ins, should be decided last since they can be used to fill in "holes" in your shelving organization.

Book Categories

Once you've been open for awhile, you will have a better idea of what genres sell best for you. Some stores sell a lot of mysteries or science fiction, while others sell an abundance of romance novels and children's books. The trends in each store are different so expect the unexpected. Within a year, you should have a good idea of what your primary customer base likes. Until then, you need to provide as much variety within each genre as possible.

The following is a list of the book sections in my store, what each section includes, how each is organized, and how many shelves the section fills. Categories are listed in rough order of popularity, though as mentioned above, keep in mind that the books that are most popular in each store will vary.

Use this as a guideline when planning your store. My store is 2,800 square feet and we have more than 150 shelf units (each shelf unit has five individual shelves and holds about 180 paperbacks or 75 hardcovers). If your space is smaller, you will have to decide how much space to devote to each genre.

Mysteries - These can be difficult to distinguish from Adventure/Suspense. Check the spine for "Mystery" to be indicated. You may have to scan the back cover for quotes from book reviews or the book description to indicate if it's "A great mystery" or a "Suspenseful tale." The authors that are quoted also help determine where a book belongs. For example, "Agatha Christie's favorite author" is probably a mystery. We separate mysteries and file them by author. Popular authors include James Patterson, Sue Grafton, and Patricia Cornwell. Seventeen units.

Adventure/Suspense – We separate mysteries and adventure/suspense, though some stores keep them together. Adventure/suspense includes legal thrillers, war, police dramas, and other action books. Popular authors include John Grisham, Tom Clancy, and Robert Ludlum. Nineteen units.

Romance Novels – Includes general romance novels. Eighteen units.

Hardcover Fiction – This section includes hardcovers and oversized paperbacks (trade paperbacks) for general fiction and adventure/suspense. Note that mystery, horror, classics, romance, and science fiction hardcovers are shelved in their respective sections. Seventeen units.

Religion and Spiritual – All religions with sub-categories including bibles and bible study, religious fiction, and hymnals. Five units.

Biographies – This section includes biographies, autobiographies, memoirs, and true stories that don't fit in any other section. Books are shelved by author. Business biographies are filed in the Business section, bios of presidents and historical figures are filed in history, and crime stories are filed in True Crime. Five units.

Science Fiction – Includes science fiction and fantasy novels, as well as anime and role-playing game books. Popular authors include Isaac Asimov, Ursula LeGuinn, and Fred Saberhagen. Twelve units.

Classics and Literature– There are many authors that belong in this category. Some are Charles Dickens, Pearl S. Buck, Nathaniel Hawthorne, Jack London, Mark Twain, Shakespeare, J.D. Salinger, etc. When in doubt, scan the book description for an indication of "Literature" or "Classic." Three units.

Kids' Corner – Kids' books are roughly organized by age (it is impossible to keep this section neat), starting with the youngest kids' books on the bottom shelves, the middle kids' (ages 7-11) on the middle shelves, and the teen books on the top shelves. Six units (designed as "Kids' Corner" and includes a basket of toys and small chairs).

Horror – These books are usually indicated on the spine as "Horror" and usually have dark/black covers and gruesome pictures. Vampire books are also classified as horror (e.g., Anne Rice). Other popular authors include Stephen King, Dean Koontz, and Clive Barker. Four units.

General Fiction – Includes regular fiction novels that are NOT mystery, adventure, romance, etc. Historical Fiction is also filed here. Popular authors include Maeve Binchy, Anita Shreve, and John Irving. Five units.

Self-Help – Includes books on self-improvement and how to improve aspects of life, filed by author. There is a separate shelf for books about relationships and a separate shelf for pure psychology books. Recovery books (Alanon, Alcoholics Anonymous, etc.) are on their own shelf in the Health section. Six units.

History – Includes military history, politics, U.S. and world history, etc. Six units.

Diet and Fitness – Includes diet and nutrition. Two units.

Health – Includes books about pills, diets, various diseases and conditions, physician's desk references, etc. Four units.

Parenting and Family Planning – Includes books on pregnancy, discipline, and parenting advice. One unit.

Audio Books – Audios for sale take up two units. Audio rentals are spread out so many can be displayed face-out and take up five units.

Cookbooks – These are separated by category: healthy cooking, international foods, entertaining, desserts, barbecue, and general. Two units.

Sciences – Includes all sciences: math, sociology, geology, astronomy, geology, philosophy, etc. Psychology is the only one that is separate (located with self-help). Three units. *NOTE* We used to carry some computer books but eliminated these since they become obsolete so quickly.

Reference – Includes dictionaries, foreign language books, maps, and atlases. Two units.

Hobbies – This section includes books on sewing, knitting, pottery, aviation, automotive, collecting, and all hobby interests. One unit.

Home Improvement – Includes books about painting, woodworking, carpentry, cleaning, organization, and decorating. Books on construction are also filed here. One unit.

Gardening – Located next to Home Improvement and includes books about plant care, vegetables, etc. One unit.

Westerns – Includes true westerns (pictures of cowboys and stories of riding the trails). Historical fiction novels (e.g., Jean Auel) are filed in General Fiction. Three units.

The Arts – This section includes sheet music, books about the music industry, books about the theater and entertainment industry, art books, art technique books (photography, painting, etc.). Two units.

Poetry – Includes all poetry collections and shares a shelving unit with short stories. ½ unit.

Short Stories – Includes short story collections such as *Chicken Soup for the Soul* and shares a shelving unit with poetry. ½ unit.

Astrology/Occult – Includes New Age, astrology, alien abductions, etc. One unit.

Collectibles – Collectible books include old volumes and signed editions and take up three units. We also have our higher priced collectibles on a shelf behind the counter.

Movie Tie-Ins – Includes books either inspired by a movie or vice versa. The spine often indicates "Movie Tie-in" or the cover shows a picture from the movie. One unit.

Travel – Includes books about specific cities, travel tips, and travel writing. Shelves are organized by region. Two units.

Sports and Games – Includes biographies of sports figures, sports stories, and instruction including baseball, golf, tennis, hiking, camping, etc. Games cover two shelves and include instructional books for gambling, card games, chess, etc. Two units.

Large Print – Includes all books printed in special enlarged text for the visually impaired. One unit.

Other Genres of Books
There are several categories of books that we decided not to carry. Here they are:

Textbooks – These have high price points, which can be attractive, but they also become obsolete very quickly. This is a good specialty business if you have a lot of space and can locate near a college where another used textbook store doesn't already exist. Otherwise, it is probably wise to avoid these. There are some exceptions. Older history, science, foreign language, and math textbooks may have some interest to your customers. Price these inexpensively and they will get scooped up.

Computer Books – Since technology is changing so quickly, most computer books are obsolete quickly. While some people may like to find a copy of a book if they are still running an older version of some software, it will require a lot of space to maintain enough variety to make it worth your while.

Harlequins and Series Romances – These sell quite well in some stores, but in my store, they just collected dust. You may want to start with some and see how it goes. Some romance authors become quite collectible, but finding these special editions can be like finding a needle in a haystack. The price point for these books is also low and we found that it just wasn't worth the shelf space.

Homeschool Books – This is another genre of books that we tested. These can do quite well if you have the space and a large community of homeschool families. Many of these families use up their budget allotment for new books and are happy to find older editions of various educational books. Unfortunately, you will need a fair amount of space to keep the amount of inventory required to make everyone happy.

Book Club Editions – Most of us have joined one of those inexpensive book clubs at one time or another. These clubs offer members substantial discounts on new books. Unfortunately, they are able to offer these low prices because they print the books on cheap paper stock. These books age quickly and can't handle the wear and tear of multiple readers. In most cases they are hardcovers, and the people who buy most hardcovers are those who want to keep them for years to come. You can identify a book club edition because it is usually a smaller than typical hardcover version and does not have a retail price. Once you handle a few of these, you will be able to spot them from a mile away. On rare occasions you may come across a current bestseller from a book club. Go ahead and accept these but price them lower than you would a regular hardcover.

Reader's Digest Editions – Reader's Digest has a popular series of books where they condense several books into one volume and sell it inexpensively. Most book store shoppers don't want condensed novels—they want the whole thing. These should be avoided or tossed into the bargain bin.

Encyclopedias – The internet has practically diminished the need for hardbound encyclopedias. It takes a lot of shelf space to keep a complete set of these on hand so unless you have a tremendous amount of space to spare, it's probably not worthwhile to keep these on hand. However, very old versions of encyclopedias—those considered collectible—could have some value. Just avoid the ones issued in the past forty years.

New Books: Friend or Foe?

There are hundreds of used book stores that survive and thrive without carrying new books. However, there are just as many that carry both. One store famous for its gargantuan size is Powell's Books in Portland, Oregon (www.powells.com). Another impressive success story can be found from Half Price Books in Dallas, Texas (www.halfpricebooks.com).

I have tested out the sale of new books and have had mixed experiences. Regional books always sell well—these are books that discuss local history. One of the leading publishers of regional books is Arcadia Publishing (www.arcadiapublishing.com). You will probably also come across several local authors who have published interesting regional guides and may be able to purchase or consign books from them directly.

Hot new titles, such as *Harry Potter* or anything currently recommended by Oprah, can also sell well. We carry dozens of books by local authors. Some don't sell at all; others sell swiftly if the author is well known in the area. Mostly we do this to support local talent and generate goodwill in the community.

Many stores stock their shelves with a mixture of new and used books. Whether or not you decide to do this could also depend on your budget. New books are expensive, though one of the greatest perks in the book industry is that in most cases, they are also returnable. If a book doesn't sell, you can ship it back to the distributor and pay only the cost of shipping.

Instead of ordering directly from publishers, most book stores order through book distributors. Distributors often have a minimum order quantity—some as high as $500. Discounts for book orders range between 35%-50% depending on the quantity ordered.

Ingram (www.ingrambook.com) is the largest and most popular distributor in the book trade, offering books in virtually every genre. There are also distributors who specialize in genres such as children's books, science guides, or textbooks. For an excellent and comprehensive list of distributors, visit www.bookmarket.com/distributors.html.

Remainder books are another option. These are overstock books that publishers liquidate to make room for new titles. Many are distinguished by a black line across the barcode or top of the book pages. These books are typically in mint condition and published within the past few years and cover a wide spectrum of genres. You won't find current bestsellers in remainder book inventories, but you can find some unique titles. Discounts for these books can be as deep as 80% off of retail, so if you have the space and think you have an audience for these, they can be worthwhile. Unfortunately, you can't return remainder books so you have to be fairly certain they will sell.

Here are some providers of remainder books:

✓ www.loveforbooks.com/default.asp
✓ www.kudzubooks.com
✓ www.wgpbooks.com/

You can also perform an internet search for "remainder books" to locate many other dealers.

Inventory Management Software and Scouting Tools

Depending on your budget and how you plan to run your store, you may want to invest in inventory management software. I don't use any software to track my inventory, but can certainly see the value in doing so and may consider this in the future.

Inventory management lets you track your inventory levels for each title. There are a variety of programs to choose from and each has different features. Many include point of sale solutions so you can integrate your inventory and check-out process. In this case, you will either link up your cash register with a computer or transform your computer into a point of sale system.

Other programs allow you to upload your inventory either onto your own website or to online booksellers such as Amazon.com.

Inventory scouting programs let you check current prices of used and collectible books from anywhere using a mobile device such as a cell phone or PDA. If you plan to scout books, these tools can save you time and money.

Here are some of the most commonly used software applications for the book industry:

Bibliopolis BookHound: http://www.bibliopolis.com/cgi-bin/biblio - Online inventory management.

HomeBase: http://www.abebooks.com/docs/homebase/main.shtml - Provided by ABE books and offers tools for managing inventory uploads, tracking customer wants, and other tools.

BookAccents: http://www.bookaccents.com/ - Inventory control and point of sale solution for book stores.

Anthology: http://www.anthology.com/ - Inventory control, point of sale, and online book sales management.

BookScoutPRO: http://www.bookscoutpro.com/ - Used for book scouting to check prices from mobile devices (PDAs and cell phones).

ScoutPal: http://www.scoutpal.com/ - Used for book scouting to check prices from mobile devices.

BookHero: http://www.bookhero.com/index.jsp - Used for book scouting to check prices from mobile devices.

Amazon.com also hosts user forums and has a handy thread for discussing third party software tools:
http://www.amazonsellercommunity.com/forums/forum.jspa?forumID=26&start=0

Section 7
Operations Procedures

Trade Policy

One advantage that a used book store has over other retail businesses is that you don't have to spend a lot of money on inventory once your store opens. Your customers should replenish your inventory through your book trade policy.

A trade policy allows customers to bring in their used books in exchange for credit toward other used books. The rate of credit offered varies greatly from store to store and city to city so you should check your competition to see what their policies are and offer something similar.

Some stores offer to buy books for cash. Whether or not you decide to do this is up to you. If your competition is doing this, you may feel forced to implement this policy. We currently do not buy books for cash since we have no shortage of books and most of our competitors don't offer this service.

Trade credit can be tracked in a number of ways. We track our credit accounts on 3x5 cards. The customer name and phone number are listed along the top line and the credit is tracked along with the date of each visit. We keep the card on file and customers simply give us their names when they come in to shop. Given the advances in technology, this is a rather old style method for tracking credit, but it works just fine.

Some stores track credit information on the computer. Others write up a credit slip and make the customer responsible for hanging on to it. Again, choose a system that works best for you.

How much credit you issue can also depend on the policies of other stores in your area. We offer 25% of retail price in credit and require customers to pay for half of their purchases in cash. For example, a customer who wants to buy a $4 book can apply $2 in credit and must pay $2 in cash. This is a great way to ensure steady cash flow.

Some stores offer pure credit exchanges and do not require customers to pay cash. This seems to be more common in stores that are well established and have been open for 10+ years. When I first opened the store I offered pure credit trades, but quickly felt like I was running a library instead of a business. Implementing the ½ cash, ½ credit policy has made a world of difference in the revenues and cash flow. Most customers understand this policy. If you encounter people who don't, simply explain that you are running a business and have to pay for its expenses. That usually turns the situation around.

Make sure your credit policy is very clear. Some stores only allow trades in the same genre. For example, someone who brings in romance books can only use their credit toward other romance books. In my opinion, this policy is a bit too complicated to manage. We simply limit credit and make it valid only toward other used books. Credit is not valid toward other merchandise, such as greeting cards or gifts. We also mark certain new or collectible books as cash-only.

The one genre we do separate is audio books. People who trade in audios can use the credit toward other audios, but regular book credit cannot be used toward audios. We keep a separate card for each customer who trades in audio books.

It's a good idea to type up your complete trade policy and post it in the window of your store. We print small fliers that outline the basics of our policy so we don't have to repeat it over and over and so we know that the rules are clear. Here it is:

Book Lovers Book Store
Book Trade Policy Overview

Credit can be redeemed at a rate of half cash/half credit. For example, to buy a $4.00 book, you can apply $2.00 in credit and must pay $2.00 in cash, plus tax.

Credit is valid toward other used books, except collectibles and books with orange price stickers. Credit is NOT valid toward other types of merchandise in the store (cards, gifts, bookmarks, audio books—unless audio books are traded). Credit is kept on file at Book Lovers.

Book Lovers accepts gently-used books in most genres. We do not accept Harlequin series books, book club editions, Reader's Digest books, text books (homeschool books okay), or any books in poor condition. Books accepted are at the discretion of the book store representative.

Book Lovers typically gives 25% of the cover price in credit. This price may vary at store representative's discretion.

Complete trade policy is posted in the store. Policy is subject to change.

*****

Book Condition

Books will come through your doors in all states of wear. I once had a guy bring in a box of books that was clearly stored in his garage—it was full of bugs! I promptly asked him to take them outside.

When you first open the store, it will be tempting to accept every single book into inventory to fill the shelves. But your shelves will fill quickly and as time goes by, you will notice that some books won't sell. Here are some things to watch for when it comes to the condition of books:

✓ Hardcovers should have dust jackets unless they are rare or collectible (though missing dust jackets will diminish their value).

✓ Ex-library books, the ones removed from circulation at the library, are usually full of library stamps and information. Again, unless they are rare books, you should probably pass on these.

✓ Outdated books such as *Finances for the '80's* or *Hot Hair Styles* printed in the 1970's will do nothing but take up space on your shelves.

✓ Loose bindings, musty-smelling tomes, and water damaged books aren't going to be hot sellers.

✓ There are two genres where condition is far less important: Western and Science Fiction. Readers of these books don't seem to mind if the paperbacks are worn and tattered—they are just happy to find these books. These are also two of the genres that are most difficult to acquire since these readers tend to keep their books forever. Eagerly accept any books from these genres, including book club editions.

Dealing with Overstock

It won't be long before you are faced with every used book store owner's nemesis: overstock. Your worst offenders will be the bestselling authors including John Grisham, Tom Clancy, and Patricia Cornwell. Before you know it, copies of books by the most popular authors will multiply like bunnies and you will have to decide it they are worth the shelf space.

I've seen crowded stores that will stock half a dozen copies of these books. Our shelves are maxed out so we limit each author to two or three copies of each book (unless the title is currently a bestseller). The rest of the copies are stored in boxes or paper shopping bags in the back room until we haul them off on our monthly trip to one of the local charities.

You will also have people who simply drop off books as if they are donating to your store. Sometimes these can be fantastic treasure chests; other times they are old boxes of junk that nobody wants. You will haul them to your storage area and be glad when they're gone. And when customers bring in books for trade and you turn some of the volumes down, they often won't want them back and will request you dispose of them.

It can seem like a huge waste to simply give away a truckload of books, but it's the only way to minimize chaos. I usually share the love by donating ours to different charities throughout the year. You will get a receipt for each donation and will likely max out the amount of charitable donations you can claim on your taxes each year.

I have also enjoyed donating books to schools. Recently, I met a teacher at a brand-new local high school who told me that they didn't yet have a library! I sent him off with a trunk-load of fiction paperbacks that he planned to distribute to the kids and the new library. I didn't even care that there was no receipt involved.

I've also mailed books to the troops overseas. Receiving a thank you note from them was one of the most rewarding experiences I've had in this business.

We also have a bargain table where we sell some of our overstock for just $1. We only offer books that are three years old or later and don't allow them to be traded back in. This is a popular attraction in the store and helps customers try out new authors, thus returning to purchase the rest of the author's regularly priced books.

Finally, I let my staff pick and keep any books they want from the overstock. They love this little perk—one of the few benefits I can afford to offer them.

You will likely resent dealing with overstock but it's a fact of life for all used book stores. Just develop a system for storing and getting rid of them each month.

Pricing Your Books

The simplest way to designate a pricing structure for used books is to cut the cover price in half—this is what we do. For example, a paperback with a retail price of $7.99 is sold for $3.99 at our store.

I've seen all kinds of pricing structures at various stores. Some cut the price in half and then add $0.30 or $0.40 to it. Most customers probably won't notice or mind this policy; it just makes it a bit harder to do the math. For hardcovers, you might want to increase or decrease the price by a dollar or two.

There are numerous ways for actually getting prices on the books. We started by writing prices on removable price stickers and sticking them on the backs of books. This worked fairly well; however, it was time consuming and expensive to purchase all those stickers. The stickers also fell off with a fair amount of handling.

Now we write prices in light pencil on the first page of every book. This way the price can easily be erased if the book is for a gift or collectible, yet it is simple to do and leaves no room for argument. We do still use orange price stickers that are removable to price new and some collectible books. This clearly indicates to our customers that the book is cash-only and cannot be purchased with trade credit.

There are a number of book inventory software programs (which we will discuss later) that can also print price stickers and scan-able bar code labels.

I have seen used book dealers who write their prices in ink on the first page. I make it a personal rule to avoid using ink inside a book. There is no reason to deface a perfectly good book by writing in ink, unless it's a mass market paperback that is on its last leg (for example, a bargain book). This will also immediately decrease the value of a collectible book and should NEVER be done!

The same is true for store stamps. Some stores like to stamp their names inside of books. I have never understood this policy! While I suppose it offers a permanent reminder of where the book came from, it also devalues the book. If getting your store name inside the book is that important to you, consider writing it in pencil next to the price. Book dealers and bibliophiles will thank you for your consideration.

Audio Book Rentals

The popularity of audio books is on the rise even given the increasing demand for downloadable formats. Most cars have either a CD or cassette player and audio books are especially popular with commuters and people on road trips.

Because audio books can be expensive to purchase, rentals offer an affordable alternative. I tell customers that renting an audio book is similar to renting a video. Instead of paying $39.99 to purchase an audio they will listen to once, customers can rent the book from us for just a few dollars.

Audio rentals have provided us with a nice steady revenue stream. To build up an initial inventory, I bought audios in bulk from eBay. I also ordered both used and new copies of newer titles from Amazon.com. You really only need a couple hundred titles to get the program launched.

You will want to print up an agreement that your customers sign to make sure they understand your return policy and their responsibility. While you can threaten to charge their credit card if an audio isn't returned on time, you could run into some legal trouble if you actually do this. If a customer defaults on the agreement, write letters and make phone calls in an effort to resolve the problem. We write off a few books each year as a loss, which costs far less than dealing with legal issues.

We track audio rentals on 4x6 index cards. They are filed by title. When an audio book is checked out, we write in the customer name and the date due and put the card in the front of the file. It's easy for us to take a quick look each day to see what books are due. I always place a friendly reminder call on a due date and remind the renter that there is a late fee of $1.50 per day. This is usually enough incentive for them to get the book back right away.

The following is our audio rental rate overview. You can use this as a template to outline your own policy.

Book Lovers Audio Book Rental Rates

Daily Rates – Per Book

Number of days is determined at the time of checkout and is prepaid. *A late fee of $1.50 per day will be assessed for all late returns.* You may extend your rental period by contacting the store prior to the due date to purchase additional plan time for your rental.

Number of Days (Prepaid)	Rental Fee
4	$5.99
7	$7.99
14	$13.99
30	$25.99

Frequent Listeners Club

For people who listen to audio books regularly (commuters, for work-outs, trips, etc.), our Frequent Listeners Club allows you to keep one or two books checked out at all times. Books may be out for up to 45 days and then exchanged for a new title upon return and within membership term. Please notify Book Lovers if books will be out longer than 45 days; otherwise, a $1.50-per-day late fee will be applied.

We will also reserve books for members of this club. Simply place your request in person or call us and we will call you when the title comes in. Reserved titles must be claimed within 24 hours of notification. Frequent Listeners Club members also receive a 10% DISCOUNT ON ALL BOOK PURCHASES at Book Lovers.

Term of Membership	Plan A One Book	Plan B Two Books
Three Months	$84	$134
Six Months	$154	$224
Twelve Months	$294	$394

Gift Certificates

Most retailers agree that gift certificates are a worthy product offering. These have a number of incentives: they bring in immediate cash, can introduce new customers to your store, and many are either never redeemed or the redeemer will spend more than the value of the certificate.

Many credit card processing companies offer credit-card-style gift cards that you can issue yourself using your card processing machine. These do have a price associated with them since you will be charged for each card your issue and again each time you swipe a card.

You can also print your own gift certificates or purchase them in bulk from a retail supply company. We print our certificates on fancy postcard paper and hand-write in the amount just like writing a check. We provide a nice envelope along with the card and they look very professional. They have been good sellers for us, especially during holidays.

Special Orders

One way to breed happy customers is to offer special orders of out-of-print books. If you have a computer at your store, offer to place orders for your customers. You would think that by now everyone is comfortable with ordering online, but this isn't true at all.

I order used books through Amazon.com and abe.com for many of my customers. I usually charge around 10% as an order fee, though you could certainly charge much more. I don't offer this service as a way to make revenue, and instead offer it more as a customer satisfaction tool.

Create a simple special order form so you can capture the customer's name and contact information, along with the price, shipping fee, and your fee. It's a good idea to have a policy that special orders are not returnable and have customers sign to indicate their acceptance.

Employees

Hiring and firing employees can be both rewarding and challenging. The biggest challenge is finding reliable and trustworthy people who can represent your business and help you keep it running smoothly.

I have had the most success in hiring right from my customer base. Customers frequently inquire about jobs and can often become your best employees since you know they already love books. Purchase a set of generic job application forms from your local office supply shop and let people fill them out, even if you're not hiring. You can keep them on file just in case the need arises.

Make sure you hold a thorough interview and check references. Many business owners make the mistake of hiring friends and this can lead to problems later on. I find it's best to stick with people you have no emotional ties to so that you keep everything fair and professional, especially if you have more than one employee.

Since you probably can't afford to offer benefits, you may want to let your staff check out books for personal reading for free. I allow my staff to read as many books as they like. If they want to keep a book or buy any other merchandise in the store, they can purchase at a discount of 30%.

It's also important to create a clear line of communication with your employees. They will appreciate knowing what is expected of them, and you also want to make sure that they feel comfortable enough to come to you with issues. Define a list of daily tasks and responsibilities so there is no question about what is expected.

Don't forget to show appreciation for your staff. Retail is not an easy business and some days will be better than others. If you have employees that go above and beyond in their efforts for you, show your thanks with a gift certificate for dinner or coffee.

Once you have a good employee or two working for you, you will realize the great advantages that they bring. You will have more time to deal with other tasks and will be grateful for those who make your job easier.

You will have to actually pay your employees, which means you will need to calculate payroll taxes and withholdings. This can be done with software, such as

Quickbooks, or can be hired out. Your local bank as well as your accountant should each offer payroll services. I pay my bookkeeper to handle payroll for me. Twice I month I send over a summary of the hours worked and she faxes me back payroll stubs for each employee. I write the checks and include the pay stubs.

My bookkeeper also prepares my monthly deposits and reminds me to take the deposit to the bank before the 15th. I find it's worth every penny to have a professional deal with these issues.

If you plan to do it yourself or want to learn more, check out the IRS Employment Tax publications: www.irs.gov/businesses/small/article/0,,id=98868,00.html.

To download the complete Employment Law Guide from the U.S. Department of Labor (DOL), visit www.dol.gov/asp/programs/guide.htm. The DOL also has a special division devoted to small business compliance. The Office of Small Business Programs can be reached directly at 1-888-9-SBREFA.

Operations Manual

An operations manual is an excellent tool for your business, especially if you plan to hire employees. By outlining your daily procedures and policies, you can empower your employees to run your business when you're not there.

It's a good idea to write your manual in a word processing program so that you can update it often when policies change—and they will continue to change. Print it out and keep it in a binder near the cash register so it's easily accessible.

The following is the actual manual that we use at the store:

Sample Operations Manual

Book Lovers Book Store Procedures Manual

Overview

The number one priority is pricing and shelving books that come in. New inventory means new sales! If there are customers in the store, try to stay near the cash register and keep the register key with you. If the store is crowded, just stay at the register and wait for it to thin out.

Please greet every customer who enters the store. Many want to browse, but if someone looks lost, offer to help find something. If we don't have what they are looking for, offer to write it down on the wish list.

*Please be sure to provide **great customer service**. Greet all customers with a smile and chat with them when they come to make a purchase. Thank each customer for his or her purchase or for coming in. The same is true for phone calls. Please be friendly and courteous to all callers.*

The clipboard behind the counter lists any new policies or notes from the person working the day before you. Please check this each day. There is also a list of things to do when it's slow.

For unusual requests or situations, use your best judgment. If you have a problem with a customer, you can always take their number and offer to have the owner call—or give them my name and have them call me. Please just leave me a note so I know to expect the call! When in doubt on any situation, please leave me a note so I can clarify a procedure.

Walk the store a couple times during the day to check for books out of place. Also check the kids' section for toys and disarray. Replace any "holes" on the display tables up front.

You can post a "Back in 5 Minutes" sign on the front door and lock it if you need a potty break!

Feel free to surf the internet and take breaks, especially when it is slow—and after all incoming books have been shelved!

Opening Procedures

- *Lock the door behind you when you enter.*
- *Disable the alarm system.*
- *Turn the door chime on: press Options twice until "Door Chime" displays, key in the code to activate.*
- *Turn on lights.*
- *Turn on heat or a/c if needed.*
- *Get the $100 starting cash from the safe and put it in the register.*
- *Turn on stereo and ceiling fans.*
- *Put sandwich board sign on curb if the weather is good.*
- *Turn "Closed" sign over to "Open" and turn on neon sign.*
- *Unlock the door and have a great day!*

Closing Procedures

- *If customers are remaining at 10 minutes to closing, feel free to let them know you are closing in 10 minutes.*
- *Do a quick run through of the store—especially kids' section—and make sure everything is neat.*
- *Make sure the store is empty and lock the front door.*
- *Turn "Open" sign over to "Closed" and turn off neon sign.*
- *Turn off heat/AC.*
- *Turn off ceiling fans and stereo.*
- *Run end-of-day sales report.*
  - *Turn cash Register key to "X" and hit **Amount Tend/Total**.*
  - *Then turn key to "Z" and hit **Amount Tend/Total**.*
- *Stack twenties and checks in top right of safe. Count out $100 in cash for the following day as follows: 25 ones ($25), 9 fives ($45), 3 tens ($30), and leave on top shelf in safe. Put the rest of the change in appropriate stack in the safe.*
- *Please check that cats have some dry food and water!*
- *Turn out lights.*
- *Set the alarm and lock up!*

Cash Register Procedures

To Make a Sale
- *Type in amount WITHOUT decimal point.*
- *Select appropriate department button.*
- *Repeat for all items.*
- *Select **Subtotal w/tax** button.*

- *Type in amount tendered and select either __Check__, __Charge,__ or __Amount Tend/Total__ for cash. The register will calculate any change due.*

To Open Cash Drawer
- *Use the __#/ST/NS__ button (No Sale button). Note: the cash register counts the number of times this button is used during the day so it is best to minimize use.*

Percentage Discount—discount ENTIRE sale—(our most common discount)
- *Enter items for sale.*
- *Subtotal sale.*
- *Type in percentage amount (for example, type in "__10__" for 10 percent) and select – __RA%__.*
- *Subtotal again and complete the sale as usual.*

Percentage Discount (single item) – *Note: discount must be entered immediately following the item*
- *Enter item for sale. DO NOT SUBTOTAL!*
- *Immediately enter discount percentage and type in percentage amount and select –__RA%__.*
- *Continue entering items for sale as usual, subtotal, and complete the sale as usual.*

Redeem a Coupon for a Specific Dollar Amount
- *Enter items for sale as usual.*
- *Subtotal the sale.*
- *Type in coupon dollar amount and select __Cpn.__*
- *Subtotal and complete sale as usual.*

Void an Item
- *Select the __Void__ key.*
- *Type in amount of item.*
- *Select the department to be voided.*
- *You can continue with the sale as usual or void additional items if voiding an entire sale. When voiding an entire sale, subtotal the voided items and hit the __Amount Tend/Total__ key to complete the sale as a negative amount.*

*If you need to void an entire sale and have a customer waiting, you can cash the sale out and void it after the customer leaves. Just don't forget to void it! Voids of entire sales should be stapled to the receipt and left in the envelope with the daily sales report.

Refund

Refunds are rare, but if a customer wants to return an item, please honor their request (unless the item is damaged). Use your best judgment in this situation and question returns of collectibles. Check for original price entry on the first page and verify the receipt. Some scammers will buy a collectible and try to return a fake copy, though (knock on wood) I haven't seen this here yet.

Processing a refund is similar to a Void:

- *Select the __Refund__ key.*
- *Type in the amount.*
- *Select the department.*
- *Subtotal and complete the sale as usual. The total should reflect a negative dollar amount.*

Apply Store Credit

- *Tally up books the customer is purchasing on the calculator.*
- *Multiply the total by 50%—deduct this amount from the customer's credit account and enter the same amount in the cash register for sale.*
- **If the customer has only a small amount of credit, simply subtract the amount of credit from the purchase total on the calculator and enter the balance in the cash register.*

Processing Credit Cards

Note: the credit card machine won't work if someone is on the phone! However, if you hang up the phone, the credit card transaction will automatically start to process.

Process a Sale

- *Swipe the credit card.*
- *Select Debit or Credit (ask the customer).*
- *Type in dollar amount and hit the green Enter key.*
- *Have the customer enter pin if necessary.*
- *The screen shows the status of the transmission.*
- *A receipt will print; tear this off. The screen asks if you want to print another copy; select Yes. Keep one copy for us and give one to the customer.*

Process a Refund or Void *(this should be extremely rare)*

- *The credit card terminal has a menu of options. Use the yellow key to scroll through the options to locate Void or Refund.*

- *The terminal will ask you for a password. Swipe the card and complete the transaction as usual.*

Audio Rentals

New customers need to fill out an audio application (located in the stacking trays behind the counter).

Locate the title of the audio rental in the card file. Write the customer's name, date out, and date due. A four-day rental is due on the fourth day. For example, a book rented on Monday will be due on Friday. Audios that are out on rental are put in the front of the file so we can track any late rentals. Late fees are $1.50 per day.

Charge the customer for the rental and let them know it can be returned after hours through the mail slot in the door. When audios are returned, mark a check on the card and re-file the card and audio book.

Gift Certificates

Gift certificates are available in any denomination. They are located in one of the front folders in the file crate behind the counter. Please write it out like a check in the amount requested and be sure to give the customer an envelope along with the certificate.

*Important: Gift certificates need to be rung up in the GIFT CERTIFICATE department because they are non-taxable! This department automatically calculates the sale as non-taxable.

To Redeem a Gift Certificate:
- *Enter the items for sale as usual and Subtotal the sale.*
- *Hit the Refund button, type in the amount of the gift certificate and select the Gift Certificate department button.*
- *Subtotal again. If there is an amount due, complete the sale as usual. If the customer has a balance remaining on the gift certificate that is more than $1.00, create a new gift certificate for the balance. For less than $1.00, simply give them change.*

Pricing Books

Prices are lightly written on the first page of the book in pencil. Price stickers on covers should be peeled off without damaging the book. Goo Gone can be used to remove *stubborn sticker glue, marks, or stains. This should only be done if the book is worth the time (don't waste the time on $2.00 paperbacks!).*

Prices should end in .99. For example, a book with a cover price of $7.99 should be priced at $3.99.

Orange price stickers are used to indicate cash-only books. These should be used for audios, collectibles, and newer/bestsellers.

Hardcovers *– ½ of List Price*
- o *Always flip through the first few pages to check for author signatures!*
- o *Hardcovers without a list price should be priced between $6.99 and $9.99, depending on the book's condition.*

Paperbacks *– ½ of List Price*
- o *Paperbacks with cover price <$1.00 should be set aside so we can check collectible status*
- o *Books should have a minimum price of $1.25.*

Children's Books *– ½ of List Price.*

Non-fiction Books *– ½ of List Price. Please set these aside so we can check online to determine if we want to sell them on the internet.*

Audio Books for Sale *– ½ of List Price. These are priced the same as regular books. If the audio doesn't have a price, it is probably a book club edition. If it's a current title, you can estimate that we will sell it for around $9.99. *Note on the customer's card if they trade in audios so we can make an exception and let them apply credit toward audio purchases.*

Processing Book Trade-ins

Our complete pricing policy is posted in the front store window. Store credit is valid toward other used books. It cannot be used toward greeting cards, gifts or other non-book merchandise, collectibles, audio books, or books marked with an orange price sticker.

We typically give 25% of cover price for books in good condition, and customers must pay half cash/half credit. For example, a customer who wants to buy a $4.00 book can apply $2.00 in credit and must pay $2.00 in cash. It is essentially a two-for-one trade, *but we require half of payment in order to maintain cash flow and pay the rent! Please explain this policy to new customers—or give them one of our fliers.*

The easiest way to tally up incoming books is to enter the cover price for each book in the calculator. For books that don't have a cover price, you will need to estimate the value. Once all the books are tallied, multiply the total by 25%. Enter the amount on the card along with the date.

Books We Don't Accept

- *Recent textbooks. The only exceptions are older textbooks about history or science.*
- *Series Romances. Anything by Harlequin, Silhouette, Regency, etc.—these are the thin $1.00-$3.00 romance subscription paperbacks.*
- *Ex-library books, unless they are in great condition and have an obscure title.*
- *Encyclopedias.*
- *Other outdated books (financial books from the 80's, etc.).*
- *Anything in poor condition (musty, dusty, dirty, water damaged, etc.).*
- *Reader's Digest condensed novels.*
- *Comic books, magazines.*

Employees

- *Employees receive a 30% discount on all purchases from Book Lovers.*
- *You are welcome to borrow a book anytime.*
- *Overstock books in the back that will be donated are freebies! Feel free to take any of these home. Note: the books on the shelves and tables in the back are internet inventory and NOT overstock!*
- *Please round time cards to the nearest 15-minute interval.*
- *Time cards are due by the 15th and the last day of each month.*
- *Paydays are on the 15th and the last day of each month. You are paid through the final day of the term. For example, payday on the 15th will be paid for the 1st through the 15th, even if you shift isn't over yet!*
- *Personal calls are fine but please keep them brief while customers are in the store.*

Cats

I will handle most of the maintenance with the cats but in case of my absence, please be sure to check their food, water, and conditions in the back room. You always have my permission to take either to a vet in an emergency. You can either pay with available cash in the store or I will reimburse you. Please be sure to contact me in the event of an emergency.

Sugar and Sweetie see:
(Dr. contact info)

Misc. Procedures

Changing Receipt Tape

The rolls of tape for the register, credit card machine, and calculator are located in back room, on the first shelf on the right.

The cash register requires thermal paper (it doesn't use an ink cartridge). The rolls should be marked for the cash register, but if not, make sure you use THERMAL paper. The larger rolls are for the cash register and the smaller rolls are for the credit card machine. The plain paper rolls are for the calculator.

For changing the tape in the register, lift the lever and drop in the roll. Close the lever down and use the FEED button to make sure the paper is running smoothly.

To change the tape in the credit card machine, press the button on the right side of the machine to open the cover. Just drop the roll in and close the cover. Use the feed button to move the paper up.

*****

Section 8
Marketing Your Business

Most of your customers will come from a 10-mile radius of your store, so you should concentrate your advertising in this area. This should also be a priority for you since you can't just turn on the "Open" sign and expect people to find you—trust me! Advertising can feel like a big expense, but remember that it is an *investment* in your business.

Phone Book Ads

The first thing you should do is call your phone company and place a phone book ad. People looking for books frequently reach for the phone book. They will also call ahead and ask you to check your stock for a certain book, or ask about store hours or directions. Phone books are only issued once a year, so it may be months before your entry makes it to print. You also don't want to miss the advertising deadline so make this call early.

There are also several phone book providers in most cities, and unfortunately you will probably need to advertise with each. A regular entry in a small phone book can run around $20 per month, while big ads can cost hundreds or even thousands of dollars. Stick with something small. You might splurge and add a little color or background to your listing in an effort to make it stand out. But the bottom line is that most of your customers will still come to you simply based on geography and you need to at least be listed in the book so they can find you.

Publicity

The best advertising you can ask for is publicity in a local newspaper or news program. To get the media's attention, you will need to send press releases with an interesting news angle. When I opened my store, my press release headline was, "Former Silicon Valley Worker Kisses Off Corporate America to Open a Used Book Store in Sacramento." This worked well and led to several news stories—free advertising! The very first big article that ran in the Sacramento Bee caused business to *double* in the month that followed.

A press release should be brief. One page is best, and two pages is a maximum. The release should include enough details so that a reporter could write a short article based solely on the information provided. The release should not be an announcement that a business or product simply exists, but should have an enticing "hook." The trick is to make the hook interesting enough to capture the attention of the reader.

Reasons for Sending a Press Release

- ✓ Grand opening
- ✓ Special event
- ✓ Anniversary
- ✓ Awards received
- ✓ Partnerships or strategic alliances
- ✓ Announcement related to upcoming holiday
- ✓ Charity event
- ✓ Results of an internal survey
- ✓ Announcing a contest
- ✓ Announcing contest winners
- ✓ New product or service and how it helps the public
- ✓ Free offer
- ✓ Expanded hours
- ✓ Change in services offered

Tips for Writing a Press Release

Be careful with your wording to avoid sounding like a sales brochure—this is sure to discourage the media from pursuing the story. Read several sample press releases before writing yours so you understand the proper format. Some good sources for reading professional releases are www.BusinessWire.com and www.PRNewswire.com. Follow these rules to write a press release that gets the attention you want:

- ✓ Start with a proper heading that includes your contact information. When listing phone numbers, indicate a day and evening number (reporters may call at odd hours) or simply list your cell phone number.

- ✓ Give the release an enticing title that captures the reader's interest and print it in **bold type**.

- ✓ Double-space the body of your release for easy reading.

- ✓ The first paragraph should include the basics of who, what, where, when, and why. You want to lay the foundation and include your hook immediately. Remember that you want to capture the attention of the media and get them excited about your story.

- ✓ Determine the purpose of your press release. Is it to announce a grand opening, special event, introduce a new product, or share valuable information with the public? Include the key points that make your story interesting.

- ✓ Use quotes from business partners, clients, or other professionals to give the story more color and credibility. As awkward as it may be, you may want to quote yourself—especially if you are the subject of the release.

- ✓ Close with a brief summary of the business or the person you are promoting.

- ✓ Do not allow grammar or spelling mistakes to sneak into a press release. Make sure you edit your writing thoroughly and have a friend—or better yet, two friends—review it for errors and content.

Sample Press Release Outline

FOR IMMEDIATE RELEASE

Business Name
Address
Contact Person
Phone
E-mail

CATCHY HEADLINE INDICATED IN BOLD CAPITAL LETTERS

Date – City, State – Lead paragraph including summary of who, what, where, and

when.

Body of press release should include three-to-six paragraphs. Include quotes from

yourself or others (make sure to get their permission). Write the content as if it were an

article you were reading in a magazine. Don't forget to double-space the text.

Paragraph Two

Paragraph Three

Paragraph Four

Paragraph Five

About the Company:

Include brief overview of company, such as the date founded and the mission of the

business.

*****

Where to Send Press Releases

You should begin compiling a list of your local media contacts—all local newspapers, including the small independent papers, as well as local radio and television stations. Most media outlets have websites where you can locate contact information. They will often list a general fax number or e-mail address where they accept press releases. They may also list individual editors or producers along with their contact information. In this case, focus on sending your release to those who cover business and lifestyles news.

You can pay a press release service, such as www.PRWeb.com, to distribute your release nationally; however, this really isn't necessary unless you want to try to attract this kind of exposure.

Printed Products and Mailers

You should have bookmarks and business cards printed with your store information to remind people to keep coming back. A mailing list is another great way to remind your existing customers to return. Collect e-mail addresses and send a monthly update to your customers (this costs you nothing!). You can also send printed newsletters through the mail, though this option does involve some added expense in copies and postage.

I started out sending a one-page newsletter to my customer database. I had them printed in black ink on pastel paper, tri-folded them, stamped them, and mailed them off without envelopes. I included details about events and new products and always included a coupon.

When the database grew significantly larger, I switched to sending postcards. I design them myself using Microsoft Publisher (they have great templates that make it easy to design these) and print them in black ink on pastel card stock. The printer then cuts each sheet into four postcards. We affix address labels (printed from our contacts database) and stamps and send them out. Since there is limited space on postcards, they are either printed with a coupon for 15% off or to announce an upcoming event. Both the newsletters and postcards always bring in plenty of customers and have proven to be worth the cost of printing and shipping. You can also apply with the post office to receive bulk mail rates.

Paid Advertising

You may want to run ads in local newspapers or publications in your area. Include a coupon with your ads to provide incentive for new customers to visit your store and also allow you to track the success of your advertisement. You will probably have to test a number of advertising strategies until you find the ones that work best for you.

I've tried a variety of paid advertising strategies with mixed results. The local newspaper has a neighborhood section that costs a bit less than a regular ad, but the cost is still quite high—typically over $100 per ad. The challenge with newspaper advertising is that for it to work effectively, you should repeat your ad numerous times. This can be cost prohibitive since a month of ads can run upwards of $500 or more.

Some of the smaller independent papers have worked well for us. We have also had good success with direct mail coupons, though again the price point is high and it takes several months to see real results. The local discount newspaper— the one that is mostly full of classified ads—fell flat and wasn't worth the effort at all.

No-Cost and Low-Cost Marketing Strategies

Here are some ways to get the most bang for the least number of bucks.

✓ **Canvas the Neighborhood** – Fliers and door hangers are a great way to advertise your business in the surrounding neighborhood. You can do this yourself or hire a teenager to distribute them.

✓ **Partner with Local Businesses** – Once you own a business, you will find yourself meeting all kinds of other business owners in the area. You can work together to co-promote each other by handing out each other's coupons or displaying fliers and business cards. We held a promotion with a local coffee shop. For a week they handed out our coupons with every purchase and we put one of their coupons in every customer's bag. The promotion cost very little and went a long way to spread exposure and bring in new customers.

✓ **Discount Cards** – Since the cost of printing business cards is so low, we've found a unique way to bring customers back month after month. I printed up a rubber stamp that says the following:

> Customer Rewards Card
> Save 10% Off Your Next Purchase
> Expires: _____

We stamp the backs of our business cards and manually write in an expiration date, usually the last day of the following month. Then we put one of these cards in every single bag with purchase. Customers love these and it gives them incentive to return in the next month or so.

✓ **Donate to Local Charities and Schools** – Offer your products or services for charity auctions and events. This will get you exposure to everyone who attends the event and build loyalty with members of the organization you are supporting. We often donate gift certificates to charity raffles and events.

✓ **Hold a Charity Event** – You can sponsor a local charity or event by hosting a collection drive for goods and cash or by offering a raffle. We held a raffle to support our local cat rescue organization and gave away a variety of prizes including autographed books donated by local authors, gift certificates for the store, and other prizes donated by businesses in the area. This was not only a rewarding endeavor, but it created a lot of goodwill with our customers and got everyone talking about the store.

✓ **Window Painting** - If you have windows in the front of your store, you can use them to attract attention from far and wide. It is surprisingly inexpensive to have your windows painted by a professional, and the end result can last a year or more, depending on how much exposure your storefront has to sunshine and weather elements. Make sure you hire a professional window painter to do the job. I've seen businesses that have tried to do this themselves and the results are never impressive.

Furry Mascots

Books and cats seem to go hand in hand (or hand in paw!). I considered adopting some store cats for awhile after opening the store and finally pulled the trigger about a year later. I'm so glad I did! I visited our local SPCA and found two mature adult cats (three and four years) that had been surrendered together and needed to be adopted together since they suffered separation anxiety. They had been in the shelter for months and everyone there was so glad to see Sugar and Sweetie finally find a home.

I had worried about how the customers would feel about store cats, but most of the worry was unfounded. 99.9% of the people who walk through the doors go straight for the cats. They are a constant source of amusement for everyone and the cats enjoy all of the attention they receive every day.

If you decide to adopt a store pet or two, there are a few considerations. First, you need to make sure to get approval from your landlord! Older cats also work a bit better since they are usually mellower than younger cats and you will worry less about destruction or behavior issues. You also need to make sure someone is able to care for and feed the animals when the store is closed on holidays.

Most animal shelters or foster parents for animals can tell you a bit about an animal's temperament. It's important to adopt animals that are going to be good with people since you are dealing with the public. I always favor animal shelters over breeders and recommend you consider this option, too. It is far more rewarding to adopt an animal in trouble than it is to pay a breeder. There is a huge pet overpopulation crisis in America and every animal that is rescued becomes one less that suffers from an untimely death.

Another option might be to provide foster care for some of the animals at your local shelter. There is a book store in Calistoga, CA that keeps a giant cage of kittens and cats in its store window and assists in finding homes for the animals. Not only is this a wonderful way to contribute to a worthy cause, but it adds to the ambiance of the store and customers love it.

I do occasionally hear from a customer who is allergic to cats. Since we take good care to vacuum and dust often, most can tolerate the store without problems as long as they don't touch the cats. I can't imagine giving up the cats just to accommodate such a small percentage of the population. They can choose to shop in our store or not, and since so many more of the customers enjoy the cats, I have no regrets whatsoever about having them there.

I also had no idea what a draw they would be to the store. Their picture is on the store website and not a week goes by without someone mentioning, "I came in just to see your cats!" I mention them in all of our advertising: "Come meet our store cats!" Several customers have even brought in gifts for the cats including beds, toys, and treats. Sugar and Sweetie have really enhanced the overall environment and make it fun for customers and employees to come to the store every day.

Book Signing Events

If you have the space and desire, book signing events can be a great vehicle for promoting your store and developing goodwill within the community. Local authors love to have the opportunity to showcase their books and often you can attract media attention for these. Our newspaper features a literary column every week and nearly every event we run gets us a mention in the paper.

For the most part, authors will come looking for you so you probably don't have to spend too much energy looking for them. However, you can contact your local writers' groups and let them know that you are available to host events.

We find that events work best on the weekends. We hold most of our events from 12 p.m. - 2 p.m. on Saturdays. We set up a folding card table at the front of the store and a chair for the author. We have the authors bring their own books and we sell them on a consignment basis, keeping 40% of the cover price.

The attendance for these events varies greatly depending on the exposure prior to the event. If the author is good with marketing and manages to get a newspaper article, radio or TV appearance prior to the book signing event, this almost always ensures a good turnout. The industry average for book signing events is for an author to sell around eight books! Not exactly an impressive number, but it's the exposure and the added activity inside the store that offers the real payoff for you.

We have also hosted several "Meet & Greet" events where we have between 15-20 local authors together on one day. These events draw all kinds of interest and most customers end up buying books from several different authors. This is another great way to get the media's attention.

If you do host book signing events, remember that it's still your store and how the event is conducted is totally up to you. You should not be expected to pay for the author's travel expenses. It's nice to offer a beverage and maybe a snack, but it certainly isn't mandatory. We simply treat the authors with respect and make sure they are comfortable.

Some authors may want to give a talk or a reading from their book. Others will sit there like a bump on a log (the worst kind). The best authors are those who are savvy with marketing, making an effort to promote the event early on and engaging the customers who show up at the store during the event.

After holding dozens of events and seeing all different kinds of authors, I implemented an application process. Not too many stores do this, but it really helps me to understand how savvy the author is and whether or not he or she will be a good fit for an event at our store. The following is a copy of the application:

Sample Book Signing Event Forms

Book Lovers Book Store
Book Signing Event Application

We receive a large number of requests for book signing events at Book Lovers. We do our best to support local authors and use this application process to evaluate event opportunities and select those that meet the needs of our customers.

We also want to make sure that we set appropriate expectations with authors. Though we do some promotion of events via our mailing list and with our media contacts, we depend on the author to make the effort to tell his/her friends and family, notify the media, and do whatever possible to ensure a successful event. The unfortunate reality is that unless your name is Tom Clancy, you can't expect many people to show up without some publicity effort.

Author Name:	
Today's Date:	
Phone Number:	
Website URL:	
Email Address:	
Book Title:	
Publisher:	
Date Published:	
Retail Price:	
Genre:	

Who is your target audience (age, sex, etc.):	
Indicate three dates you are available for an event:	
Recent or upcoming book signing event dates and locations:	
Have you read our "Book Signing Event Overview" document?	

Brief description of book (150 words or fewer):

How will you help promote your book signing event at Book Lovers?

Any reviews, awards, media coverage, or other recognition we should know about? This isn't mandatory, so don't worry if you don't have any yet!

Do you plan to speak, give a reading, or other type of presentation? (This is not required.)

Other details you would like to share:

Thank you again for taking the time to complete the application process. Please return the completed application to <e-mail address> or drop it off at the store. We will review the details and get back to you within two weeks. If you don't hear back from us by then, you are welcome to send us an e-mail.

*****

In addition to the application, I also give each author a copy of our Book Signing Event Overview so they know what to expect. This is definitely above and beyond what most book stores do, but the way I see it, it benefits both our store and the author. Here is a copy:

Book Lovers Book Signing Event Overview

Thank you for your interest in participating in a book signing event at Book Lovers Book Store! We do our best to support local authors and appreciate your time and effort.

Scheduling:
We prefer to schedule events at least one month in advance to allow enough time for promotion. We like to schedule the events on Saturdays from 12 p.m. - 2 p.m., but we can be flexible if there is another time that works for you.

We have had good success with dual-author events. If you have a writer friend or colleague that you would like to share the spotlight with, please let us know. We may also choose to schedule you along with another author who has a book in a similar genre. Please let us know if you have any concerns about this.

Promotion Efforts:
We will do our best to promote your event via our website calendar, store newsletter, and by notifying local events calendars. Please be sure to send us any press kit information or at the very least, a copy of the book with a written description of any information you would like to include at least ONE MONTH PRIOR TO THE EVENT.

If you plan to send your own press release, please be sure to include the following details:

Book Lovers Book Store
<address> <phone> <website>

Keep in mind that timing is everything in the media—they love stories of a timely nature. If you have a book for moms, we should schedule your event around Mother's Day. If you have a book about relationships, Valentine's Day might be a good time. The key is to find a great hook whenever possible to increase the chances of getting media coverage.

What You Can Expect from Us:
We will set up a table at the front of the book store and help you display your books. Feel free to bring along any promotional material including posters, reviews, visual aids, etc. If you have posters, please drop them off at the store at least two weeks prior to the event so we can start creating a buzz!

We have a restroom that you can use (it is not available to the general public) and we can offer you bottled water. You are welcome to bring along coffee or anything that makes you more comfortable.

For New Authors:
If this is your first book signing, we would like to help set your expectations. It is unlikely that there will be a line out the door (trust us—we would like that just as much as you would)! Industry standards indicate that the average number of books sold at a signing event is eight copies. In our experience, new authors may sell even less than that, especially if there hasn't been any significant promotion effort.

Unfortunately, book signings are not necessarily the best place to sell books, but they are great for getting the word out, networking, and getting some experience with the public. If you are able to get media attention, this can be a tremendous help.

What You Can Do:
- ✓ Tell everyone you know (e-mail works great)! Help create a buzz and invite your friends and family. It is particularly helpful to have your fans there at noon when the event begins to build excitement with the walk-in customers.
- ✓ Contact the media. Let them know about your book and your event. Find a great "hook" for your media announcement. Contact the appropriate editor for your subject matter. For example, if you have a business book, contact the business editor.

✓ Post fliers about your event at your office, school, church, and anywhere else you can.

Local Media Outlets:
✓ The Sacramento Bee: www.sacramentobee.com
✓ Fox 40 News: http://www.tribune.com
✓ Sacramento News & Review (e-mail): sactonewstips@newsreview.com
✓ Carmichael Times (e-mail): editor@carmichaeltimes.com
✓ Capital Radio (e-mail): news@capradio.org
✓ KDVS Davis College Radio (e-mail): news@kdvs.org
✓ KFBK (e-mail): kfbknews@clearchannel.com
✓ KVMR: http://www.kvmr.org/
✓ The Zone Radio (e-mail): marshallp@radiozone.com
✓ The End Radio: http://www.endonline.com/contact/
✓ 98 Rock: http://krxq.net/station/
✓ V101.1: http://www.v1011fm.com/pages/programming.html
✓ News 10 Good Morning: goodmorning@news10.net
✓ KCRA 3: http://www.thekcrachannel.com/news/
✓ Good Evening Sacramento-UPN (e-mail): goodevening@upn31.com
✓ Senior Spectrum: www.senior-spectrum.com
✓ Sacramento Magazine: www.sacmag.com

*Note: If there is a community newspaper in the city where you live, be sure to get in touch with the editor! Local papers love to feature stories of nearby residents.

Tips for a More Successful Event:
Since you will be sitting at the front of the store, you should try to greet people with a smile and a simple "Hello" when they enter. Customers can be shy and may be interested in what you're doing but afraid to approach you. When they ask about your book, give a brief overview and be prepared to answer questions. You might ask a question to engage them in conversation and gauge their interest. Be careful not to place a "hard sell" since this can turn a potential buyer off. Instead, simply present your book and be as friendly as possible. If the customer says, "Well, I don't read thrillers," you could try suggesting, "Well, what about your husband or father? This would make a great gift!"

Money, Money, Money:
We typically receive 40% of the book sale price. Authors should bring enough books to supply the event and this number can vary. We've had event sales

range from zero to 80 copies, so please be prepared for anything. You are also welcome to bring a dozen books in prior to the event. We will fill out a standard consignment agreement and get them on display as soon as possible.

During the event, we prefer to keep the books behind the counter so when someone would like one signed, they should pay first then return to you with the book for signing. We will keep track of the number of books sold and will complete a sales summary form at the end of the event. You can expect to receive a check no later than 14 days after the event.

Recommended Reading:

I am often asked for advice on book promotion so here are some books that I've read and enjoyed:

- ✓ *Jump Start Your Book Sales* by Tom and Marilyn Ross
- ✓ *1001 Ways to Market Your Books* by John Kremer

Store Overview:

If you aren't yet familiar with Book Lovers, the store is approximately 2,800 square feet and houses 30,000+ used books. We carry some new books, mostly by local authors. It is not a typical used book store! You will find that it is bright, clean, and organized. We also sell gift items, greeting cards, and posters.

Foot traffic in the store varies but Saturday is usually the busiest day of the week. Sometimes we have twenty people browsing the aisles; other times there may only be one or two. We never know what to expect from one day to the next since Murphy's Law dictates that everything is unpredictable. Weather can also be a factor, although some of our busiest days are when it rains. The moral of the story: just be prepared for anything!

We will do our best to make you feel welcome and make the event a fun experience for you! Again, I want to emphasize how much we appreciate you and look forward to spending a fun afternoon with you!

Please contact me with additional questions.

Best regards,
Stephanie Chandler
Owner & Chief Book Officer

*****

Section 9
Website and Internet Sales

I am always surprised when any business today does not utilize the World Wide Web. It has become very affordable to host a website and most hosting providers offer tools that make it easy to get online.

Though a website is not crucial to your business, it does provide another method for new customers to find you. It can also allow you to communicate with your existing customers since you can post special event notices or encourage people to sign up for your mailing list. If you're technically savvy, you may even consider selling books directly from your site.

Domain Registration and Hosting Services

Yahoo: http://smallbusiness.yahoo.com/ — This is the service that I use. Plans start at just $12 per month and include dozens of e-mail addresses, tools to track activity on your site, and a variety of marketing options.

Go Daddy: www.godaddy.com – An inexpensive service with plans starting at just a few dollars per month.

Network Solutions: www.networksolutions.com – A reliable hosting provider from a company that has been in business for years.

Website Design

You can hire a website designer or tackle this task yourself. Most web hosting providers offer free templates that you can easily modify to meet your needs. If you want a more sophisticated site and have some computer skills, consider using Microsoft FrontPage or Adobe Dreamweaver to design and manage your site. You can also opt to purchase an inexpensive template that can be modified with either of these programs.

Your website can include as much or as little information as you like. Here are some ideas:

- ✓ Description of your store
- ✓ List of products available
- ✓ Address and contact information
- ✓ Map and/or directions
- ✓ Hours of operation
- ✓ Clips of any media coverage you have received
- ✓ Pictures of the store interior and exterior
- ✓ Events calendar
- ✓ Community resources

Visit some of your competitors' sites to get some ideas about what you want to include.

Online Sales

If you are computer savvy, selling online could be a good option for you. It's also a great way to dip your toe into the bookselling business, since you can start by selling from home long before your brick and mortar store is open.

Selling online can give your brick and mortar store an additional source of income and a way to quickly turn over collectible and hard-to-find titles. While this isn't mandatory for used booksellers, it's a strategy that has served me well. And as the book market becomes more competitive, it's my opinion that every used book store should be taking advantage of online revenues.

Many online booksellers treat their storefronts as a storage place for their internet books. Internet book sales can generate significant revenues if done correctly. One strategy that worked quite well for me was hiring an employee specifically to handle internet book sales. I paid him commission on his sales, which provided him plenty of incentive to hunt though our substantial inventory and locate the gems.

I keep track of my inventory with a simple Excel spreadsheet. As I list a book for sale, I enter the title, author and price in the spreadsheet. When the book sells, I mark it sold, enter the shipping cost, deduct Amazon's commission and calculate my profit.

I personally don't like to co-mingle my storefront books with my internet inventory. I keep my internet inventory in the back storage room, alphabetized by title. This makes it easy to locate the books when it's time to ship and I don't have to worry about my online inventory walking out the door. I'm sure there are plenty of booksellers who would disagree with my strategy and would put their internet inventory right in with the rest of their storefront inventory. If this works for you, great! I worry about my online feedback ratings and try to avoid misplacing books or having them be handled too much, altering the condition.

There are six main venues for selling books online:

Amazon.com - The largest online bookseller also boasts steady site traffic and makes it relatively easy to get started with their seller program.
www.amazon.com/exec/obidos/tg/browse/-/1161232/102-0477539-2803347

ABE.com – This site is a popular destination for people who want to buy or sell collectible books. ABE also offers its sellers free inventory management software that most book dealers love, and books listed for sale here can also be automatically listed for sale on Barnes and Noble's website and Amazon.com. www.abebooks.com/docs/Sell/

Alibris.com – This site has gained popularity over the years and books listed here can also be automatically listed on Amazon.com and BarnesandNoble.com. http://sellers.alibris.com/why.cfm

Half.com – This is owned by eBay and is a popular site with the younger market demographic due to the fact that they also offer textbooks and music for sale. http://half.ebay.com/help/sell.cfm

eBay – The largest online auction dealer is also working to integrate book sales from Half.com into its offerings. EBay can be a good place to sell some collectible titles and large quantities of books. Because of the saturation of sellers on eBay, prices can be degraded, so be sure to research items before listing them for sale. www.ebay.com

What Sells Well Online

I'm going to save you some time and money by sharing a few tips on what books sell well online and what to avoid.

Most popular fiction titles will NOT sell well online. Because of the large print runs, sometimes in the hundreds of thousands, the market becomes saturated and these books can sell for as little as $0.01. The exception to this rule is less popular fiction or books that were issued in small print runs and then went out of print, thus making them rare or hard to find.

This same rule applies to popular non-fiction. If the book was previously on the bestseller list, it has probably lost its value.

The books that retain their value best are those that are more obscure. I always check the prices online for interesting non-fiction titles. For example, here are some items currently listed in my Amazon inventory:

- ✓ *Rustic Adornment for Homes of Taste*, $19.97
- ✓ *Chinese Erotic Art*, $24.97
- ✓ *20 Centuries of Great Preaching*, $28.97

✓ *Dragons and Nightmares*, $9.99
✓ *Gems and Minerals of America*, $12.97

Collectible and autographed books can also command big bucks online. Always make sure to thumb through the first few pages of each book to see if it's autographed. You might be surprised by how often you will come across these.

You will eventually develop a sense for what sells well. The best strategy is to simply login and check prices online. Since you also have a storefront, if a book doesn't have enough value online, you can simply price it and stick it on your shelves for sale.

How the Process Works
First of all, decide what price point is worth your time. Unless you are selling huge quantities of books online, it probably isn't worth your time to list books for $1. I have a policy to never sell anything worth less than $5, though many stores will tell you that it's worth their time to sell off cheaper stock.

When you list a book for sale through an online book store, your listing will be displayed under the available used books. To maximize sales, you will want to write a comprehensive description of the book you are listing. Here is an example:

"Hardcover with dust jacket, published by Wiley 2002, dust jacket has minor shelf wear, text is clean and unmarked."

You will have to rate the condition of each book that you list. Be sure to gauge the condition accurately so you set the appropriate expectations with the buyer. For example, you never want to indicate a book is in "Like New Condition" if it has been damaged in any way. Each online book dealer lists criteria for defining the condition, so follow their guidelines and you should minimize customer complaints and returns.

When it comes to setting your price, lower is better. If you list your books manually—one at a time—you can look to see what other book dealers are charging and the condition of the available books. Your books will sell much faster if you offer the lowest price. Don't bother with pricing significantly lower than you competitors; even a few pennies can make the difference in obtaining a quick sale.

Most of the book stores also collect payment from buyers and will simply send you an e-mail when a book has sold. You are then responsible for packaging and shipping the book, typically within two business days. You should include an invoice, and may also want to include a bookmark or more information about your store.

You will likely receive payments from the bookseller on a monthly basis. Most will automatically deposit to your bank account and will deduct their fees. Each book store retains a different percentage from sales, so be sure to compare services and understand how much profit margin will be left over.

Each store should offer management tools also allow you to login to your account, track sales, and view the feedback you receive from buyers. This is also where you can issue refunds in the event that you can't locate a book in your inventory or you receive a returned item.

Shipping

You will want to set up a process to streamline shipping when you start selling books online. Trekking to the post office every day can be a waste of time and an exercise in patience. You should be seeing your mail carrier every day and he or she can pick up any number of outgoing packages.

You will need a postage scale and a way to print postage yourself. One online service, www.stamps.com, provides you with a free scale along with the ability to print postage yourself. Another provider that offers postage services is www.endicia.com.

In most cases you can ship books via media mail. This is a special fourth-class mail rate that is used specifically for books and other media. The delivery time is usually longer because it is fourth-class; however, the cost is significantly lower than first-class mail or overnight delivery.

Shipping supplies can be expensive so be sure to shop around for the best price. You will get a better deal if you order in large quantities. I use padded bubble mailers and order them from the following sources:

✓ www.uline.com
✓ www.papermart.com
✓ www.ebay.com

Section 10
Carpe Diem: Seize Your Book Store!

A used book store can be a wonderful business if you are motivated and willing to work hard to get it up and running. Don't be afraid to ask for help. In fact, I *recommend* asking for help. Before I opened my store, I used the internet to locate used book stores all over the country. I wrote to dozens of store owners, explained that I was planning to open a store in California (far away from them so I wouldn't be viewed as competition), and I asked lots of questions. More than half of the owners I contacted wrote back and shared some valuable advice.

I also made it a point, and continue to do so, to visit used book stores everywhere I go. I love to see how other stores operate. If the owner is present, I take a moment to introduce myself and compliment him on a job well done. And I always make sure to support the business by buying at least one book—that's just good karma. I get a lot of inspiration and ideas from other stores.

Speaking of other stores, there is no reason why you can't make friends with your competition. Though they probably won't throw you a welcome to the neighborhood party, you can and should find ways to work together.

There will be many times when customers will ask you to recommend other stores in the area. This will be much easier for all involved if you're willing to share customers with each other. Most avid readers will visit multiple stores anyway, and as long as you have set yourself apart from your competition, you shouldn't be afraid of losing customers forever.

I have a rapport with every store in my area. This has served us all well. I love it when a customer tells me that one of my competitors referred them to me. It makes it that much easier to return the favor. You can also swap stacks of business cards with each other. Your customers will appreciate that you all work together.

I am often asked what I think have been the keys to my success as a book store owner. Here's my best answer:

✓ **Lots of Preparation.** I took plenty of time planning out my store and learning how to run a business.

✓ **Money in the Bank.** I saved and had backup funding options available.

✓ **Strive to Be Unique.** I knew from day one that I wanted my store to be different. I worked on giving it a warm and friendly feeling. I painted the walls in a bright shade of yellow, kept the aisles wide, and the shelves neat and organized. My goal has always been for my customers to say, "What a great book store!" I still love to hear that, and fortunately, I still hear it often.

✓ **Great Staff.** I can honestly say that I couldn't run my business effectively without my employees. In my case, I didn't want to be a full-time presence at the store and knew that I would need a great staff to help me execute my vision. Fortunately, the people who work for me understand the vision and keep things running smoothly. It makes it a lot easier to sleep at night.

✓ **Ongoing Marketing.** You can't expect people to just find your business; you have to tell them about it, and continue telling them about it over and over. Several years into this business, we still see brand-new faces walk into the store every single day. Most say, "I've been meaning to stop by here" or worse, "I had no idea you were here." I keep finding innovative ways to get the word out there and ultimately the efforts pay off.

Tasks to Complete Worksheet

Use this list of suggested tasks to help you build a timeline around your business planning process. Use the extra space to add your own tasks to the list.

Task Description	Target Completion Date	Date Completed
Take a business startup class at the local college, adult learning center, or small business administration.		
Read at least three business books (business startup and marketing guides).		
Interview at least three book store owners.		
Name your business.		
Design a website.		
Obtain a logo.		
Determine a business structure (sole proprietor, partnership, or corporation).		
Evaluate personal budget.		
Write a business plan.		
Locate financing.		
Begin acquiring inventory.		
Create a list of startup supplies with budget.		
Apply for business licenses and permits.		
Open a business checking account.		
Select a location and begin setting up shop.		
Set a target opening date.		
Obtain business tools (computer, cash register, fixtures, office equipment, etc.).		
Order business stationary (business cards, brochures, fliers, letterhead, etc.).		

Task Description	Target Completion Date	Date Completed
Create an operations manual.		
Hire employees.		
Plan a grand opening event.		
Send press releases.		
Turn on the OPEN sign.		
Revisit the business plan quarterly.		

Additional Tasks:

Additional Resources

Trade Associations

Joining a trade association can have many advantages. Each association offers different benefits including discounts on products and services, access to vendors, networking opportunities, industry statistics, newsletters and other publications, and many more.

- ✓ American Booksellers Association: http://www.bookweb.org/
- ✓ American Wholesale Booksellers Association: http://www.awba.com/
- ✓ Antiquarian Booksellers Association of America: http://abaa.org/
- ✓ Antiquarian Booksellers Association (International): http://www.aba.org.uk/
- ✓ Antiquarian Booksellers Association of Canada: http://www.abac.org/
- ✓ Association of Booksellers for Children: http://www.abfc.com/
- ✓ Australian Booksellers Association: http://www.aba.org.au/
- ✓ Booksellers Association of the U.K. and Ireland: http://www.booksellers.org.uk/
- ✓ Canadian Booksellers Association: http://www.cbabook.org/main/default.asp
- ✓ Christian Booksellers Association: http://www.cbaonline.org/
- ✓ Florida Antiquarian Booksellers Association: http://www.floridabooksellers.com/
- ✓ Georgia Antiquarian Booksellers Association: http://www.gaba.net/
- ✓ Independent Online Booksellers Association: http://www.ioba.org/
- ✓ Independent Mystery Booksellers Association: http://www.mysterybooksellers.com/
- ✓ Maine Antiquarian Booksellers: http://www.mainebooksellers.org/
- ✓ Midwest Booksellers Association: http://www.abookaday.com/
- ✓ New Atlantic Independent Booksellers Association: http://www.newatlanticbooks.com/
- ✓ New Hampshire Antiquarian Booksellers Association: http://www.nhaba.org/

✓ Northern California Independent Booksellers Association: http://www.nciba.com/

✓ Pacific Northwest Booksellers Association: http://www.pnba.org/

✓ Southern California Booksellers Association: http://www.scbabooks.org/home.html

✓ Washington Antiquarian Booksellers Association: http://www.wababooks.com/

Miscellaneous Resources

✓ Library of Congress Book Fairs and Literary Events: http://www.loc.gov/loc/cfbook/bookfair.html

✓ Library of Congress (information on book repair and preservation): http://www.loc.gov/preserv/

✓ Book Expo America (largest annual book industry event): www.bookexpoamerica.com

✓ Tony's Tips (useful advice from a successful book store owner): http://www.bookrack.org/accents/Tony_s_Tips.htm

✓ Information on book collecting from About.com: http://classiclit.about.com/od/bookcollecting/

Appendix: Sample Business Plan

This is the original business plan I wrote for Book Lovers. It's a bit wordy and could probably be chopped in half. You'll notice that some of the policies and procedures changed since opening. I provide this to you as an example of a plan, though it's certainly not the only option! Your plan should reflect your own plans and style. You may also find the case studies and anecdotal stories to be interesting and potentially useful when creating your plan.

Book Lovers Book Store
Gently Used Books & Audio Book Rentals
Business Plan

"Success doesn't come to you... You go to it."
-Marva Collins

Executive Summary

The purpose of this business plan is to describe the future business operations of Book Lovers Book Store, as well as to use this document as a tool for planning and understanding the details of the business.

Mission:
Book Lovers will open a retail location of 2,000-2,500 square feet to sell "gently used" books and small gift items. Customers will be able to trade their used books for store credit. The store will have a sense of community by displaying works of local artists, allowing customers and local businesses to advertise on the bulletin board, and by holding community events such as children's book readings, poetry readings, and book signings.

Book Lovers will be a clean, well-lit, and inviting place for customers to spend time browsing. The staff will be friendly and will assist customers in locating any book they are seeking, even if it means an extensive book search via the internet. Customers will always receive a friendly greeting in the store and will be encouraged to participate in store events and email mailing lists.

Book Lovers will NOT be a dingy, dusty used book store. It will NOT be over-crowded, messy, or in disarray as many used book stores are. Book Lovers will have a strong belief in customer service, and the staff will be trained appropriately. The store will be a comfortable place that will create a repeat and regular customer base based on the quality and selection of books and gifts.

Business Overview

Book Lovers will operate as a used book store. The inventory will include gently used and collectible books. The store will also carry small gift items such as bookmarks, magnets, journals, and greeting cards. The store will buy and sell used books with the general public. Book Lovers will also host an internet used-book business, which is already in operation (www.BookLoversCafe.com), and will resell used books through such channels as Amazon.com, Half.com, and eBay.

Audio book rentals will also be available to customers. Audio books are popular with commuters, retirees, and people who listen to a Walkman while working out. Several rental plans will be offered and inventory investment is minimal in comparison with the return.

The business will be incorporated by its owner, Stephanie Chandler. Book Lovers will be open 7 days per week, depending on the foot traffic and demand. During the week, the hours of operation will depend on location. For the purposes of conservative planning, I am assuming hours of 9 a.m. - 6 p.m.

Keys to Success:
The concept of a used book store may not sound lucrative to the average person; however, the information I have found suggests the opposite. Since the inventory costs of used books are so low (typically around 10% - 20% of the book's retail value), there is room for significant profit. My research concludes that there are several keys to success and the following are the tenets that Book Lovers will adhere to:

Book Lovers Tenets

- **Excellent Customer Service** is the number one priority at Book Lovers. The staff will be trained to be friendly by greeting customers when they enter, offering assistance, and ensuring that customer expectations are not only met, but are exceeded.

- **Books Will Be of the Highest Quality**. Since the store will buy and trade books with the public, inventory will come through the door in the hands of customers every day. Only the best book dealers accept the good, clean books and are experienced enough to turn away the aging or overstocked copies.

- **Inventory Offers a Wide Selection of Titles and Genres**. Many stores will display 5 or even 10 copies of the same book because they have taken in too many in trade. Good book dealers will stop taking these in, or will unload them on the internet and make room on their shelves for other titles that are more likely to generate a profit.

- **Book Lovers Is a Clean and Inviting Store**. Many used book stores fail to present an organized shop and it is baffling to understand how they manage to turn a profit. Truly successful stores don't stack books on the floor, and they offer proper lighting and ventilation.

- **Inventory Changes Quickly So the Store Always Has Something New to Offer**. Since new inventory will be abundant from customers who bring in their books for trade, the inventory should constantly be "fresh." Special sales can be held to move slow-selling books, a bargain bin can be stocked with titles that need to move, and excess inventory can be sold off on the internet. The slow-selling titles must be cleared to make room for the popular books that ultimately generate significantly higher revenues.

The Used Book Business Defined

A used book store has some surprising advantages over a new store such as Borders or Barnes and Noble. Publishers generate thousands of new books each year, and because of this, even the largest new book store can't offer every title ever printed. In fact, these giant stores *only stock about 2% of all books ever published*.

Used book stores have the advantage of variety and selection. There are literally hundreds of thousands of book titles that have circulated through the market. Many of them go out of print, even though there are people who still want to read them. Some go out of print and become even more sought after because they reach "collectible" status. A clean first edition copy of once popular books, such as *War and Peace* or *The Hobbit*, can sell for thousands of dollars.

Inventory is easy to acquire in a retail location because it walks into the store with customers. Many people don't want to keep the books they've read. Often, they give books to libraries or simply discard them in a dumpster. People who discover used book stores also discover a place to part with their excess books. Other sources of acquiring inventory for used book sales include thrift stores, storage and estate auctions, garage sales, local classified ads, and by networking with friends and family.

The Tri-Valley Herald ran an article on 11/8/02 titled "Doing Volumes: Not every book store is losing money," and written by Rori Laverty, staff writer. Here are a few excerpts:

"It's a tough time to be an independent bookseller. The economy's still weak, Barnes & Noble, Borders and Amazon.com are extending their dominance and TV, the Internet and video games lure readers away.

For small book stores, that sounds like an automatic blueprint for bankruptcy, right? But not all booksellers in the East Bay and Peninsula are feeling the pinch. Several, in fact, say they're doing just fine.

Among the long, winding aisles at Gray Wolf Book Store on East 14th Street in San Leandro, for example, the customers keep shuffling around, just as they have for the past decade – peering through dim light at dog-eared, used books set two-deep on ceiling-high stacks of vintage orange crates.

The chefs come for the 1940s Swedish cookbooks. The amateur mechanics Come for the 1987 Datsun operating manuals. Every customer has their peculiar interest, and they keep coming back, whether it's for the free Saturday morning coffee or the chance to sit a spell and read without being rushed to a register.

While most booksellers agree the overall retail market is bleak, stores such as Gray Wolf that have an "edge" - whether it's a browser-friendly ambience, a healthy mail-order business or an intense focus on a particular literary genre - are doing more than staying alive: They're prospering.

"The difference is that this is a browser's book store, not one of these drive-throughs," says Karen von Glahn, who co-owned Gray Wolf with her husband George, who died last summer. "You have to have a little time when you come in here. But that's why people come. We have doctors and tech people who say they come in here to escape from the fast pace of their lives."

Perhaps the most successful of the local independents this year is M is for Mystery, another large and airy store on Third Avenue in San Mateo, full of (you guessed it) mystery and crime novels. Whatever they're doing is working, because the store isn't just prospering - it's having the best year in its 6-year history.

"There are so many vacant stores around here that we're getting fewer shoppers just walking in," says owner Ed Kaufman. "But the reason we're doing very well anyway is that... we're a destination store, meaning people drive here just for us. They also come in for our author events, and we ship quite a lot of books all over the country."

With the difficult economy, discount stores are thriving. Ross and Target stores continue to report earnings that beat expectations. The most successful "Dot Com" business to date, eBay, also continues to exceed its earnings expectations quarter after quarter. Meanwhile, regular retail stores are suffering from a slow economy. Used book dealers report that business remains steady or is increasing, despite the reports of reduced consumer spending.

Internet Operations

Both Amazon.com and Barnes and Noble operate successful online book stores. They have also opened up a new channel for used book dealers by allowing their network of affiliates to resell books on their sites. This model caused many people to wonder why these big mainstream companies would allow their competition to steal business out from under them. The business model is actually brilliant.

When Amazon sells a used book, it charges a commission fee to the seller and shaves off part of the shipping charge from the buyer. The used bookseller makes a tidy profit while Amazon saves costs by not having the expense involved in stocking or shipping the book. Since this program was released, Amazon's used book sales have grown steadily and attribute to a significant part of Amazon's profit margin. This has been so successful that you can now buy books on the subject of "How to Resell Used Books on Amazon.com."

Ebay and its subsidiary, Half.com, have also opened up a profitable avenue for booksellers. Half.com allows the general public to sell used books and other merchandise and takes just a small commission on each sale. Ebay is a great place to buy or sell unique or collectible books, as well as books in quantity. Many booksellers dispose of excess inventory by selling it in lots on eBay.

Aside from the above and commonly known internet book sites, there are scores of other sites where books can be bought and sold around the world. The large network of book dealers can post "wants," where they list specific books that their customers are seeking. A used book dealer in California may commonly sell books to dealers in the UK or Australia. The dealer in California may also purchase special copies of books from dealers in other countries to meet a customer request.

Current Internet Operations

In 2002 I began selling books on the internet and intend to develop this into a substantial part of my business. There are many people who operate internet book stores from their homes and do so quite successfully. The advantage of having a retail storefront is having an additional avenue for profit, and an excellent way to build inventory as customers bring in their discarded books.

Since I have been working full time to date, I have had minimal time to focus on my internet sales while also developing my business plans and researching my brick and mortar business. However, even given the small amount of time I have been devoting to these sales (about two or three hours per week), I am already generating about $150+ per week in sales.

While I obviously could not live on this kind of income, it serves to prove that there is a substantial business to be made online. I now understand the trends of what sells best and what doesn't sell, and I have begun building a solid reputation in the internet community. Because of this, Book Lovers is poised to have the internet sales take off as soon as I am able to devote full attention to listing inventory for sale.

I already have processes in place for tracking the internet sales, packaging the items, and marketing to the customers. I had rubber stamps made to speed the processes, an internet postage machine to avoid lines at the post office, and I insert a bookmark into each purchase, thanking the customer for their business and promoting future sales. Each book is carefully packaged and shipped quickly to ensure customer satisfaction.

Marketing Strategy

The following are some tag lines that Book Lovers will use in various marketing strategies:

"A Reader's Paradise"
"Gently Used Books and Audio Book Rentals"
"Meet your friends or make some at Book Lovers"
"Not your average book store"
"Escape the chaos of you day at Book Lovers"
"Books can take you to wonderful places"
"Book Lovers – Your escape from Reality TV!"

Before the doors of Book Lovers are even opened, I will send letters to local publications including The Sacramento Bee, Sacramento Magazine, Fair Oaks Observer, Carmichael Times, Gold River News, and The Sacramento Gazette. I will also write to the local television and radio stations asking that they feature Book Lovers as a public interest story. It is my hope that they will find my story, **"Woman Abandons Lucrative Tech Career to Sell Used Books,"** compelling and will give me some free PR as a result.

Grand Opening

I will also host a Grand Opening one to two weeks after a soft opening (to allow time to ensure things are running smoothly). Prior to the grand opening, a mailer will be sent out to the nearby neighborhoods announcing the event and offering special discounts. A large Grand Opening banner and balloons will be used to promote the event over the span of a weekend. Customers who attend will receive special attention and will draw discount coupons out of a special basket offering 15%-40% savings on their purchases that weekend. In the Kids' Cove section of the store, we will offer coloring books and story readings to entertain them while their parents shop.

On-Going Marketing Strategy

Book Lovers will **advertise in as many of the local publications** as budget will allow. The initial intent is to invest $200 per month to market the store and evaluate what is the most effective strategy.

I have many creative ideas for marketing that cost little or no money at all. I will visit **local complementary businesses**, such as the Music Exchange, Retirement Communities, Schools and Day Care Facilities to offer shared marketing. These businesses can post fliers and business cards in my store in exchange for the same opportunity in their stores. I will also leverage my many friends and contacts in the community, many of whom are business owners and belong to various organizations, to help spread the word and locate new venues for advertising.

Community Focus:

It is important that Book Lovers has a community focus, which I believe will also help attract customers and build loyalty. There will be a **bulletin board** displayed in the store in which customers and local business can post information for free (upon receiving my approval). The board will display local events as well as Book Lovers Events.

I will also host **children's reading** hours in the store. These are popular at some of the large retail book stores because it is a free and fun activity for parents and their children. The advantage of attending reading sessions in a smaller store such as Book Lovers is that parents can shop while their children are entertained with a story. In a larger store, parents are discouraged from leaving their children because the size of the store is so large. Not only will the parents have an opportunity to buy books for themselves at this time, but they will also become familiar with the large children's section in the store.

Through the internet, I have compiled a list of over 50 **community associations** along with contact information. Some of the associations are:

- *UC Davis Faculty Association*
- *Books in Color (Art)*
- *Les Beaux Arts Club*
- *Les Belles Artes Club*
- *Straight Out Scribes*
- *ZICA Creative Arts Literary Guild*
- *Sacramento Business Network*
- *Association of University Women*
- *Sacramento Women in Community Service*
- *Women's Civic Improvement Club of Sacramento*
- *Sacramento Poetry Center*
- *SPAM – Sacramento Poetry Art and Music Organization*

There are a number of ways to utilize this list of organizations and associations. I will seek to **share marketing** with them via newsletters and e-mail marketing. I will also inquire about events that Book Lovers could sponsor by **donating books** or advertising. This is also a great way to **network** and seek other creative ways to market the business. Members can also receive special discounts or purchase gift certificates at reduced prices.

The check-out counter will host a guest book where customers can sign up for the Book Lovers mailing list. Customers can provide either a home address, or preferably, an e-mail address. E-mail marketing is absolutely free and an effective tool, provided people volunteer to receive correspondence. Simple **newsletters will be sent out bi-monthly,** describing store events, sales, and book reviews. The store community board will also solicit articles for the newsletter from the customers themselves in hopes of further building the sense of community at Book Lovers. This letter would be another vehicle for leveraging advertising from local businesses.

Book Lovers will allow customers to fill out a short **"Reader Recommendation" card** that describes why they liked a particular title. These cards can be tucked inside the covers of inventory on display and used a tool to show other customers that a book received a good review from a fellow reader. I believe this will be a valuable tool to promote sales.

Additional Store Promotions and Tools

- *Frequent shopper cards* - Customers will receive a card to track their spending in the store. Once they have spent $50 in books, they will receive $5 off of their next book purchase. I have not seen any other used book store in the Sacramento area offer something like this.

- *Bookmarks* - A bookmark will be tucked inside each customer's purchase with details about the store operating hours and website address. The bookmark will serve as a simple and inexpensive marketing tool.

- *"Authors on Writing" Sessions* - Book signings are common in book stores and there are a number of California authors that are willing to spend an hour or two in any book store willing to promote their book. However, lesser-known authors may not necessarily draw a very good crowd for book signings alone. I located an article about a used book store in Massachusetts. After too many book signings with low attendance, the store started asking authors to give a short discussion along with the signing session. The discussions included such topics as "How I Became an Author," "Getting Published," "Writing Mysteries," etc. The store owner promoted these sessions at the local colleges and received overwhelming response.

- *Promotions with Non-Profits* - Book Lovers can provide services to non-profit organizations by offering books as rewards for service. For example, an agency may want a way to reward volunteers for 50 hours of community service. A package of books could be given away to the member, and this could be part of a public award ceremony, or written about in the newsletter.

- *Community Street Fairs* - Events such as Art in the Park and harvest festivals draw huge local crowds. I would like to rent a booth at a couple of these summer events to offer books for sale and promote the store. It is relatively inexpensive to rent a booth, typically around $100, so I think this would be a worthy experiment in marketing, and I will seek events that are close to the actual store location.

- *Free Gift with Purchase* - This idea came from an article about how to market a book store. The article suggests partnering with local businesses to make this work. For example, Book Lovers could host a promotion for

"Buy 3 Cookbooks, receive a $5 gift certificate for Bonnie's Kitchen Gadgets." Conversely, Bonnie's Kitchen Gadgets would host the promotion as "Spend $30 and receive a $5 gift certificate for Cookbooks at Book Lovers." The key to success here is to find appropriate businesses with a cross-promotional interest.

- *Common Use Products* - Another way to leverage local businesses is to create a package of related items that can be sold at each of the participating businesses. For example, create a "Get In Shape" package with a fitness book, fitness class coupons from the local gym, low-fat treats from the local gourmet shop, and a workout tape from the video store. Another example is a "Women's Treat-Yourself" package that includes a couple of novels, some scented lotions and bubble bath from the local bath shop, gourmet tea bags from the local coffee house, candies from the gourmet shop, and a gift certificate for the local beauty spa.

- *Internet Marketing* – Internet marketing is possible with many of the examples and organizations listed above. I would like to exchange internet advertising with other local business websites.

- *Book Drives* – This idea came from a used book store owner I met online. The book drives would work by having the children bring in their family's discarded books and deposit them in a donation bin at school. The school would be paid for each book collected and at the same time, Book Lovers would gain valuable marketing with the children and their parents. Books need to be purchased on an ongoing basis anyway, and whether the store pays walk-in customers or a school for books, the cost is the same.

Customer Profile

The customer profile for Book Lovers spans several groups of people. **Students** of all ages are common used book store visitors since they seek books for study and pleasure. Book Lovers will advertise at the local colleges, which, fortunately in the Sacramento area includes at least a dozen community, specialty, and state colleges.

Retirees are also typical used book store customers. Many of them are on a fixed income and like that they can purchase books at a fair price. This demographic is also interested in reading books that aren't necessarily new. Since they also have time on their hands, they can often read two to three books per week. We will target these customers by advertising with the local retirement communities and clubs. We will also offer a senior citizen discount on Tuesdays.

Book collectors frequent used book stores. Similar to other collectible items such as sports cards, stamps, and dolls, used books have a strong collectible market. A storefront is an opportunity to bring in other used book lovers (known in the industry as bibliophiles), as well as independent book dealers. These people enjoy "the thrill of the hunt" and can be expected to spend hours in used stores browsing the merchandise. Bibliophiles take joy in flipping through the pages of a potential treasure, checking to see when it was printed, if it is a first edition, and if the copy happens to be signed. A surprising number of discarded books are signed copies. In my own experience, I have "found" at least a dozen signed copies by accident over the past two years. Bibliophiles enjoy the whole experience of a book, much like musicians who enjoy sampling different kinds of music. To reach this group, Book Lovers will advertise with the annual Antiquarian Book Show held yearly in Sacramento. The Book Lovers website will also have a strong internet presence and true book collectors will seek us out.

My research also indicates that people who have completed some form of higher education are often literary types as well. To appeal to this group, Book Lovers will advertise in the nearby upper-middle class neighborhoods with targeted mailers.

Charitable Contributions

It is important to me that the store is involved in charitable activities and donations. There will be a permanent **donation bin for children's literacy**, so that people can donate children's books, which I will then distribute to various organizations. Children's books are abundant and easy to part with as children grow, so I expect this to be a successful project.

In the "Community Corner" area, I plan to work with the **Sacramento SPCA** and the **Animal Rescue Foundation** to advertise dogs and cats that need homes, as well as SPCA requests for volunteers and special events.

I will also keep an open mind to other charitable events and opportunities, as I believe it is important to give back to the community. Since there is a marketing aspect to working with charities, it is a win/win situation for both the charities and the store.

Competition and Location Considerations

There are at least 20 used book stores in the Sacramento area; however, this is not deemed to be a threat. Like antique stores, used book stores are each filled with their own unique treasures. It may actually be beneficial to be in an area concentrated with book stores. If you consider antique stores, there are many places where antique stores open their doors side by side with other antique stores. This actually generates business.

In Mountain View, California, the downtown main street (Castro Street) has four book stores. One store offers only new books, one sells spiritual books, one is a small used book store, and one is at least 5,000 square feet of used books. These have all operated on the same three blocks for as long as I can remember. And if you consider the high rents of the Bay Area, these stores have to be doing well to continue business on Mountain View's most popular street.

This same theory applies to the perceived competition of Borders or Barnes and Noble. I would happily open my doors right next to one of these giants. I am sure my business would thrive. While we share our customers because they are all readers, we also offer different specialties. Book Lovers will not have all of the newest releases; however, you also can't rent an audio book at Borders and you definitely can't find a first edition, signed Judy Blume book at Borders either.

Book Lovers will be set apart from other used book stores. I addressed this in an earlier section of this plan when I described that Book Lovers will be clean, well-lit, and organized. The fact that so many stores operate under disarray tells me that anyone can *make a living* with used books. Book Lovers will be better than that—it will be *successful*.

Pricing Strategy

The books in the store will typically be priced at half of their retail value, which is usually published on the book cover. If a book does not have a published price, it will be manually priced at a fair value. Collectible books will also be priced according to market value that can be determined by checking prices on the internet.

Many older trade paperbacks, such as Romance novels, Westerns, and Science Fiction are still popular even though their original retail price published on the cover is $0.25 - $1.00. Because of this, the store will have a policy of a $1.00 minimum book price.

The internet book sales will have a different pricing scheme based on the demand of the online marketplace. The online marketplace can see used book prices range from 25% - 500% of their retail value, depending on the market saturation of the title, or the book's collectible status. When pricing these books on Amazon.com, I will check against the other books listed to determine the price point as I do when I list them for sale today. The pricing of these books is also based on the condition of the book, so if a book were in poor condition, it would be listed at a lower price.

Books listed for sale on eBay will also have a range of values. In some cases, book lots can be lucrative. For example, if the store has multiple titles of books in inventory, these can be grouped into a book lot and sold in quantity on eBay.

There are a number of ways to market items on eBay. Romance novels, which I expect to have in abundance in the store, can be grouped together in a lot of 10 or 12 and sold on eBay to an avid Romance reader for a fair price. Collectible books can also do well on eBay, and while eBay is an auction format, a reserve price can be set as a minimum amount for a given sale. I anticipate using eBay as a tool for clearing out inventory that is not moving quickly, as well as marketing different types of book lots. Audio books will be priced for sale at 25% off of their cover price.

Store Layout

The store will be designed to hold a maximum capacity of books without seeming overcrowded. It is important that the layout is open and inviting, and does not create a sense of claustrophobia as many used book stores do. There will be books lining the walls and organized in "nooks." Please see the appendix of this document for a drawing of a sample layout.

Display tables, rotating racks, and carts will be used to market books for sale. There will be a bargain rack to move slow-selling inventory. Risers will be used to draw attention to key titles, and themes will be used in displays and rotated often.

The store will be equipped with proper lighting so that it is easy to read. Careful attention will be paid to maintaining dust levels, since dust is inherent with used books. Since book quality will be carefully evaluated, the store will not have a musty odor like many antiquarian stores. The store will be well ventilated and extremely clean.

Careful attention will also be paid to the general décor. As decorating is a hobby of mine, my intention is to create a warm environment. The general color scheme will be beige with burgundy and green accent colors. Throw pillows and potted plants will be added for accents. The windows will have thoughtful book displays that will change often and will feature themes such as holidays, sports, children, pets, etc. Inexpensive artwork will be displayed on available wall space, and the children's area will have a small table for children to color pre-copied coloring book pages. These pages will also be posted on the wall of the children's area with parental approval. Book reviews and articles of interest will also be neatly displayed on either bulletin boards or in picture frames or protective covers.

Inventory

Most publications on the subject of used book stores recommend a starting inventory of 8,000-10,000 books at a minimum. The initial inventory for Book Lovers will consist of roughly 30,000 books, all of which have already been purchased and are currently in storage. Books will be organized by category on the shelves of Book Lovers and alphabetized by author name.

Greeting card vendors have already been selected for the store and several revolving racks will display these items, along with bookmarks, blank journals, and other stationery.

I already have 300 audio books. A monthly investment will be made to add new titles to rental inventory. Customers will also bring these in for trade from their personal collection.

The following details the book categories and planned percentages of the inventory:

Category	% of Inventory	# of Books
Art	0.50%	150
Astrology	0.50%	150
Audio	1.33%	400
Biography	1.33%	400
Business	1.67%	500
Children	6.00%	1800
Classics	1.00%	300
Collectibles	0.83%	250
Computer	0.67%	200
Cooking	0.83%	250
Ethnic	0.33%	100
Family Planning	0.67%	200
Fiction	18.33%	5500
Finance	1.33%	400
Foreign Language	0.33%	100
Health and Fitness	1.17%	350
History	1.00%	300
Household	1.33%	400
Humor	1.00%	300
Large Print	1.00%	300
Local Interest	0.33%	100
Music	0.50%	150
Mystery	6.67%	2000
New Releases	0.33%	100
Non-Fiction	1.00%	300
Parenting	1.17%	350
People Are Talking About	0.33%	100
Pets	0.67%	200
Philosophy	0.33%	100
Poetry	0.67%	200
Psychology	1.00%	300
Reference	1.00%	300
Religion	0.33%	100
Romance Novels	10.00%	3000
Romance Series	6.67%	2000
Science	1.17%	350
Science Fiction	10.00%	3000
Self Help	3.33%	1000
Sports	1.67%	500
Suspense	6.67%	2000
Theater and Drama	0.67%	200
Travel and Geography	1.00%	300
War Fiction	1.67%	500
War Non-Fiction	1.00%	300
Women's Interest	0.67%	200
Totals:	**100.00%**	**30000**

Operating Procedures

An Operating Procedures manual will be developed for employees of Book Lovers soon after store opening. A general outline of procedures is as follows:

Book Operations Overview:

- On a daily basis, general cleanliness should be monitored. Make sure shelves are free of dust, check shelves for disorganized or out-of-place books.
- When customer traffic is light, take the opportunity to list books for internet sales. Use a cart to select titles for internet inventory and once they are listed, file in appropriate order in back room (internet inventory will be kept separate from main store inventory).
- Slow times are also the best time to package books for shipping and handle internet orders. If there is no slow period in a day, one clerk should be designated to work in the back room to package and ship the internet orders.
- Remember to greet every customer who walks in the door. Smile! Ask if they need help locating something, and offer assistance. Remember that the customer is our number one priority.
- When ringing up a customer sale, ask the customer if they found everything they were looking for. If not, ask for details and write down any titles they are seeking. Offer to locate the book for them and obtain their contact information and a general idea of what they are willing to spend. Also take the opportunity to mention any upcoming store events and ask if the customer has tried the "Best mocha in town."
- Cash drops should be made to the safe several times per day. The cash drawer should never have more than $200.
- When purchasing a customer's books, be friendly even if the customer isn't. If there are books that are unacceptable for Book Lovers inventory, explain this to the customer in a friendly manner. If the customer doesn't want to take the books back, offer to donate them. If they are worthy of donating, put them in the bin in the back. If they are damaged or dirty, discard immediately. All books arriving daily should be immediately displayed on the New Arrivals shelf or moved to the back for pricing and stocking.
- All new inventories in the back should be priced frequently and moved to the shelves at least once each day. Clean up any imperfections on the

books. Set aside any books that look collectible and check for values later. Keep adding fresh inventory to the shelves!

- Bathrooms should be monitored by all employees hourly. When any Book Lovers employee uses the restroom, please address any cleanup that is required. Restock soap or paper products if needed, make sure trash is in its designated container, and general restroom appearance is clean.
- All special book orders should be reviewed daily. Use the internet search tools to locate any special requests. If you locate an item that has a higher price than the customer offered to pay, contact the customer and explain the situation. Even if they decide not to purchase the book at the higher price, they will appreciate the effort.
- At store closing, scan all aisles for clutter or out-of-place books. Make sure the store looks neat and organized for the next morning.
- Close out the cash register with the daily log and deposit funds in the safe. Restock the cash drawer with the designated amount of change.
- The floors should be vacuumed and mopped each night after closing.
- Check restrooms for cleanliness and to ensure all customers have left the store.
- Turn off lights, set the alarm, and lock up!

Buy – Sell – Trade Policy:

The following policy will be posted in the book store area of the store:

Book Trading Policy

Paperbacks, Non-Fiction Hardbacks (Cookbooks, Gardening, Reference, etc.) and Audio Books

Most paperbacks traded for store credit will receive 15% of the cover price in store credit, which can be used toward the purchase of books.

25% trade value may be offered for bestsellers or books that are difficult to stock.

Books traded for cash will receive 10% of the cover price.

Hardbacks – General Fiction

These books can only be traded for store credit and will receive 10% of the cover price toward the purchase of books in the same category. We cannot offer cash for hardback books unless they are rare, current bestsellers, or hard to find.

Book Quality

Book Lovers sells gently used books in good or better condition. Books will be considered for trade if they meet the following criteria:

- *Cover and all pages are intact and in good condition.*
- *Books must not have any water damage, mold, mites, or any unusual odor.*
- *Books must not have missing or torn pages, highlighting to text, stains, or excessive wear.*
- *Hardcover books must have original dust jacket.*

Book Lovers reserves the right to decline books. Please do not take it personally. We may simply be overstocked on an item, the condition may not meet our standards, or the clerk may feel that the book does not have an appropriate resale value.

We appreciate our customers and will gladly answer any questions you may have about this policy. Thank you for your business!

****

All trade credits will be issued in the form of a receipt to customers. Customers may choose to save their credit value for use at a later date and must present the receipt in order to use their credit.

Personnel

Book Lovers will hire one to two employees after store opening. We will seek to hire retirees or college students, as both of these demographics are attracted to working in book stores. The qualities I will look for include enthusiasm, personality, a responsible work history, and a general interest in books. I don't want to hire people who only plan to be around for a few months. Thorough interviews will be conducted and references will be checked.

Summary

I sincerely hope that this business plan conveys the thought, planning, and work I have put into Book Lovers, as well as my ability to operate this business. I firmly believe that there is no reward without risk, and I realize that embarking on this business venture will be one of the biggest risks I have ever taken. I am giving up a lucrative career in technology, and I'm sure many of my colleagues will wonder if I am making the right decision. I also think that secretly, many of them will envy my decision. Regardless, this is a business I am passionate about and I am completely committed to making it a grand success.

Appendix

Case Studies

People magazine has recently featured several used book store success stories. **Half Price Books** in Texas opened its doors in 1972 in an effort to save trees by recycling used books. The founders stocked the shelves with 200 books from their own personal collections. Since then, the family-owned business has grown to 72 locations in 11 states. The 2001 sales were a whopping $98 million, and *sales growth for 2001 was up 22.5%*. The store expanded its business to some wholesale and discount books as well as gift items. The interior of the stores still has a small-business feel since the furniture and fixtures are mostly secondhand or made by the employees.

Powell's in Portland, Oregon opened its doors in 1971. Today there are 7 stores in the Portland area, including one store that spans an entire city block and contains over 1 million books. Powell's sells used, collectible, and some new books. *Sales for 2001 grew 25.7% to $44 million.* Powell's features reading hours and sells books online.

The largest independent used book store on record is **Strand Book Store** in Manhattan. The store has an inventory in excess of 2.5 million used books with a reported $20 million in annual revenue, and the space was recently expanded to 120,000 square feet. Strand is operated by Nancy Bass, who inherited the store from her grandfather. Because of its location in Manhattan, many Hollywood stars frequent the store, and a stream of revenue has been generated by renting books to movie sets, including Meg Ryan's book store in *You've Got Mail* and the law books seen in *A Beautiful Mind*.

About the Author

Stephanie Chandler is an author of several business and marketing books including

- *LEAP! 101 Ways to Grow Your Business* (Career Press)

- *From Entrepreneur to Infopreneur: Make Money with Books, eBooks and Information Products* (John Wiley & Sons)

- *The Author's Guide to Building an Online Platform: Leveraging the Internet to Sell More Books* (Quill Driver)

- *The Business Startup Checklist and Planning Guide: Seize Your Entrepreneurial Dreams!*

A frequent speaker at business events and on the radio, Stephanie has been featured in *Entrepreneur Magazine*, BusinessWeek, Inc.com, *Wired* magazine, and many other media outlets. She is also the founder and CEO of Authority Publishing, which provides custom publishing services for non-fiction books.

Visit her sites:
- Custom Book Publishing and Author Marketing: www.AuthorityPublishing.com
- Author and Speaker Information: www.StephanieChandler.com
- Resources for Entrepreneurs: www.BusinessInfoGuide.com
- Blog: www.BusinessInfoGuide.com/blog
- Twitter: http://Twitter.com/bizauthor